The Workplace of the Future

The Fourth Industrial Revolution is a global development that shows no signs of slowing down. In his book, *The Workplace of the Future: The Fourth Industrial Revolution, the Precariat and the Death of Hierarchies*, Jon-Arild Johannessen sets a chilling vision of how robots and artificial intelligence will completely disrupt and transform working life.

The author contests that once the dust has settled from the Fourth Industrial Revolution, workplaces and professions will be unrecognizable and we will see the rise of a new social class: the precariat. We will live side by side with the 'working poor' – people who have several jobs, but still can't make ends meet. There will be a small salaried elite consisting of innovation and knowledge workers. Slightly further into the future, there will be a major transformation in professional environments. Johannessen also presents a typology for the precariat, the uncertain work that is created and develops a framework for the working poor, as well as for future innovation and knowledge workers, and sets out a new structure for the social hierarchy.

A fascinating and thought-provoking insight into the impact of the Fourth Industrial Revolution, *The Workplace of the Future* will be of interest to professionals and academics alike. The book is particularly suited to academic courses in management, economy, political science and social sciences.

Jon-Arild Johannessen is a full professor in Leadership at Nord University, Norway, and Kristiania University College, Norway.

Routledge Studies in the Economics of Innovation

The Routledge Studies in the Economics of Innovation series is our home for comprehensive yet accessible texts on the current thinking in the field. These cutting-edge, upper-level scholarly studies and edited collections bring together robust theories from a wide range of individual disciplines and provide in-depth studies of existing and emerging approaches to innovation, and the implications of such for the global economy.

Automation, Innovation and Economic Crisis
Surviving the Fourth Industrial Revolution
Jon-Arild Johannessen

The Economic Philosophy of the Internet of Things
James Juniper

The Workplace of the Future
The Fourth Industrial Revolution, the Precariat and the Death of Hierarchies
Jon-Arild Johannessen

For more information about this series, please visit: www.routledge.com/Routledge-Studies-in-the-Economics-of-Innovation/book-series/ECONINN

The Workplace of the Future

The Fourth Industrial Revolution, the
Precariat and the Death of Hierarchies

Jon-Arild Johannessen

Routledge
Taylor & Francis Group

LONDON AND NEW YORK

First published 2019
by Routledge
2 Park Square, Milton Park, Abingdon, Oxon OX14 4RN

and by Routledge
52 Vanderbilt Avenue, New York, NY 10017

First issued in paperback 2020

Routledge is an imprint of the Taylor & Francis Group, an informa business

British Library Cataloguing-in-Publication Data
A catalogue record for this book is available from the British Library

Library of Congress Cataloging-in-Publication Data
A catalog record has been requested for this book

ISBN 13: 978-0-36-758484-9 (pbk)
ISBN 13: 978-1-138-33920-0 (hbk)

Typeset in Times New Roman
by Integra Software Services Pvt. Ltd.

Contents

5   Concepts   94

Foreword

This book is about how robots and artificial intelligence will completely transform working life. Once the dust has settled from the Fourth Industrial Revolution, workplaces and professions will be unrecognizable. A new class is seeing the light of day: the precariat. We will live side by side with the 'working poor' – people who have several jobs, but still can't make ends meet. There will be a small salaried élite consisting of innovation and knowledge workers. Workplaces will be unrecognizable. Robots will have destroyed bureaucratic hierarchies and torn apart the middle classes. What will remain will be contract workers with insecure jobs. We are seeing the emergence of a new class of pyjama-workers – people who can do their jobs in bed or alternatively at a café table. Slightly further into the future, we can see a major transformation in professional environments. Doctors will be medical engineers, nurses will be nursing assistants accompanied by robots. Teachers will be replaced by robots and holograms. And taking this scenario further, we see the downfall of the great dinosaurs. Metaphorically speaking, major hospitals may in these robotized times metaphorically be seen as 'burger-van hospitals', where robots diagnose, prescribe and make surgical interventions. If decision-makers stick their heads in the sand like ostriches, the sandstorm will bury the ostriches so that they never get their tiny heads out of the sand.

Our challenges and problems are not linked to finding solutions to the consequences of robots and artificial intelligence. What is difficult is to discard our engrained ways of understanding the concepts of work, casual labour, being at one's workplace, and everything that is linked to the ways in which the industrial society organizes and manages work. Those woodchips you got from the oak you sawed down: can't you glue them back together to resurrect the old tree? The point of this metaphor is that what is gone is still present in our collective memory, and that is what is difficult to change.

Although the industrial society caused the middle classes to grow and live in greater comfort, there is much to suggest that the Fourth Industrial Revolution will decimate the middle classes.

1 The workplace of the future

Introduction

This chapter is intended as a roadmap to explain what lies ahead for businesses and institutions, given the development of robots, informats and artificial intelligence.

We know that most jobs will change extremely rapidly. Until now, people who are educated have been able to find jobs. In the future, many people will not find jobs even though they are educated (Kessler, 2017). It seems likely that most jobs will be those either at the bottom or the top of the wage scale.[1]

Robots,[2] artificial intelligence and informats[3] are destroying bureaucracies and hierarchies. This hypothesis is based on the research of Abd (2017), Wilson (2017), Ross (2016), and Susskind and Susskind (2015).

The second hypothesis on which this chapter is based is as follows: robots and informatization are transferring surpluses from income from employment to investment income. A good deal of empirical research supports this hypothesis.[4]

The hypothesis reveals a paradox: productivity increases, the level of innovation increases, but at the same time average salary levels decline (McAffee & Brynjolfsson, 2017).

In the USA, it is projected that 50 per cent of today's workplaces will be automated and robotized over the next 20 years (Avent, 2016: 1–4). Robotization will take place in all occupations: journalism, teaching, medicine, defence, architecture, dentistry, the service sector, transport, the merchant navy, marketing, industry, etc. (McAffee & Brynjolfsson, 2017). The last major period of automation affected jobs in industry, during which a combination of industrial robots and global wage competition decimated millions of industrial jobs and transferred many jobs from high-cost countries to low-cost countries. It appears that the next round of automation will affect jobs in the service sector. According to two Oxford professors who conducted a major study of more than 700 different service-sector occupations, half of all jobs in the American service sector are in danger of disappearing (Frey & Osborne, 2013). Although robotization is transforming most workplaces, it is also leading to fewer work-related injuries, fewer traffic accidents, better medical diagnostics, and higher quality medical and surgical interventions. Robotization will improve the everyday quality of life of sick and disabled people and those who are otherwise in need of care. Deaf people will also find their everyday lives improved by new nano-robots and other disabled people will experience improvements. According to Ross (2016: 42), robotization is a global net benefit.[5]

In an organization such as described above, the old 'hamster-wheel mentality' will be replaced by the flexibility of the panther and the feeding instinct. All panther-type organizations will be directly engaged in competition for customers, not only those organizations that are in immediate contact with customers (Susskind & Susskind, 2015). Workers in these organizations may be described as **knowledge workers** and **innovation workers**. They will have completed a long series of specialized educational programmes, including Master's degrees and doctorates (Trot, 2015: 23; Wilson, 2017).

In a panther-type organization, everyone will be committed, motivated and focused on the customers. These are 'the survivors' in the organizations of the future. However, those who do not adopt this attitude will quickly fall by the wayside. In order for the organization to do what it is designed to do, it will be dependent on buying or leasing in many functions. These functions will be performed by the new contract workers, the same people who were employed previously in the organization and existed within its bureaucracy and hierarchy (Shipler, 2005). These people will now be 'in-sourced' by the organization on short- or long-term contracts. These new-style organizations may be 'the company of one' (Lane, 2011). These will be people who have a high level of expertise within one or a small number of areas, which they sell to one or more businesses. Metaphorically speaking, we might envisage a swarm of insects around a honey pot. These insects compete on cost and expertise in order to land contracts with businesses. We can envisage wage competition strongly depressing the price of their labour because people who want to sell their cutting-edge expertise to businesses can be found everywhere in the global economy (Banki, 2015). Geographical proximity will no longer be a factor when seeking a high level of competence combined with good availability and reliability at the lowest possible cost (Garud et al., 2002; Gaskarth, 2015). The people who will tend increasingly to sell their expertise to businesses through temporary contracts will be members of what is known as the **precariat**[6] (Standing, 2014a, 2014b). The precariat is a direct and intentional consequence of neoliberal economic ideology (Banki, 2015; Johnson, 2015b: 1).

From the 1970s onwards, the new ideology was dominated by flexibility and competition, which gradually came to permeate all aspects of the social system (Standing, 2014a: 1). Accordingly, risk and insecurity became part of employees' everyday lives. According to Standing (2014a: 1–4), this development means that millions of workers around the world no longer have stable employment prospects – the neoliberal agenda has created a political monster.

Members of the precariat perform insecure jobs. According to Standing (2014a: 1–4), the precariat is a specific social class that is developing worldwide. Many of its members are frustrated, angry and bitter at the élite who have put them in the positions in which they find themselves.

In the working life of the future, many, indeed very many, people – some estimates suggest 30–40 per cent of the workforce – will lose their jobs (Shipler, 2005; Wacquant, 2009a, 2009b). These people are referred to as the **working poor** (Shipler, 2005). This group consists of low-paid service workers and people on welfare benefits, to mention some groups (Shipler, 2005).

The new panther organizations will be extremely cost-effective and have very high levels of productivity (Murphy, 2016). They will also be good at problem-solving, have little staff turnover, and have creative and satisfied employees (Boxall & Purcell, 2010). These very well-paid employees will find their work meaningful. They will be living out their dreams in the panther organizations, and will have contacts among the precariat who can perform short-term contractual assignments (Brynjolfsson & McAfee, 2011, 2014). This kind of relationship will contribute to securing the future of 'the company of one'. Within a panther organization, the employees will flourish using their expertise to perform their specialized knowledge tasks (Bruce & Crook, 2015). These employees will be optimistic, positive individuals who will spend much of their working lives in contact with their global competence networks (Reinmoell & Reinmoeller, 2015). Those who do not succeed in making this transformation will have been forced to leave the organization and will number among either the precariat or the working poor.

Knowledge workers and innovation workers will be the relatively privileged employees in the Fourth Industrial Revolution (Murphy, 2016; Trot, 2015: 23). Murphy has, however, omitted the people who missed the bus: the working poor and the precariat. To make this kind of organization possible, with robots taking over many job-related functions and making decisions based on efficient algorithms and artificial intelligence, many or perhaps most people will have to spend most of their 'working lives' outside such organizations, existing as sub-contractors working on insecure contracts (Standing, 2014a; Johnson, 2015b).

What is happening at the dawn of the Fourth Industrial Revolution is a total transformation of the nature of income-generating work (Gans, 2016). The driving forces behind this transformation are robotization, informatization, artificial intelligence, and an extreme focus on cost-efficiency due to global competition and growing individualization (Savage, 2015; Wilson, 2017).

The main question that we are exploring in this chapter is as follows: How does the workplace of the future constitute an aspect of the Fourth Industrial Revolution?

In order to respond to this main research question, we have broken it down into three sub-questions:

1. How does the precariat constitute an aspect of the Fourth Industrial Revolution?
2. How do the working poor constitute an aspect of the Fourth Industrial Revolution?
3. How do knowledge workers and innovation workers constitute an aspect of the Fourth Industrial Revolution?

This introduction is visualized in Figure 1.1, which also illustrates how we have structured this chapter.

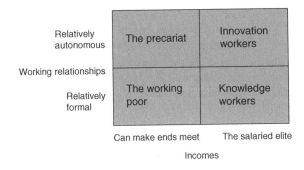

Figure 1.1 A typology of working life in the future.

The precariat

Description

In his research, Guy Standing (2014a, 2014b) has identified a new class that he calls the precariat, which has emerged through globalization, liberalization, and increasing robotization and digitization. This class has the potential to change how businesses are organized in the future and how societies develop (Johnson, 2015b: 1–4). Many activist groups from the precariat have fought for better working conditions, and both pay and job security, so they can plan the future for themselves and their families better (De Sario, 2007: 21–39; Tarrow, 2005; Johnson, 2015b).

The precariat, as the term is used here, is associated with Standing's research (2014a, 2014b), the studies carried out by Johnson (2015a) in Italy and Arnold's studies (Arnold, 2013) of insecure work in Vietnam. Furthermore, we also refer to the studies of Armano and Murgia (2015) of work flexibilization in the USA, as well as Ross's (2009) studies of insecure work in the USA. In addition, we refer to Lodovici and Semenza's (2012) studies of high-skilled youth in Europe who, despite their higher education, have insecure work and expectations of insecurity in future work relations.

We have developed a typology of the precariat in order to gain a better understanding of this phenomenon. We have divided the precariat into four types. We term the first type the **underemployed**. These are people with a good education and relatively long experience from working life. They are exposed to competition in the global economy and threatened by robotization, so their wages are pushed downwards (Arnold & Bongiovi, 2013: 290). The feeling of being excluded makes these people feel frustrated, alienated and angry (Johnson, 2015b). The underemployed are hired on short-term contracts depending on the company's needs. The examples here are many. For instance, an underemployed person could be a young legal professional who takes on extra jobs in the hope of getting a permanent job, but is not rewarded for his or her extra efforts. He or she must wait until a permanent position becomes available. However, when the position does become available there are hundreds of applicants for the position, who have also taken on extra jobs in order to gain recognition (Standing, 2014a: 33–34).

The second type is a young person with a relatively good education, but who only has temporary underpaid jobs. These young people are skilled but have not had the opportunity to gain experience in the sector relevant to their education. They have been told that it pays to get an education. Consequently, they have completed so-called mid-level higher education, often up to a Bachelor's degree. However, after completing their education they encounter a job market where they are unable to find regular well-paid jobs. We call this type the **underpaid**. These workers are also frustrated and angry, because they had expectations of a good job after graduation, but encountered a reality that was different from what they had been told to expect. Their anger may be explained as a crisis of expectation, i.e. the promises that these people are given when they work extra are merely a *fata morgana* – a mirage, an imaginary hope of a permanent job – because it is more profitable for companies to hire people on short-term contracts than to give them permanent positions.

However, despair does not necessarily lead to political action – it might just as well lead to passivity and apathy. On the other hand, Standing (2014a: viii) says that the rebellion lies in the self-awareness of the precariat as a class: 'Across the world, there is an energy building around the precariat.'

The third category is made up of people with specialist expertise, often at the Master's or PhD level. These people may have had well-paid jobs before being rendered superfluous by robotization, automation, flexibilization, digitization, informatization and so on (Garud et al., 2002). Such people often establish their own businesses: 'the company of one' (Lane, 2011). They use these businesses to sell their expertise to larger organizations. We refer to these people as **knowledge entrepreneurs**. In general, these people are satisfied with their entrepreneurial situations. They are hired on short-term contracts by larger companies, large consultancies or organizations in the public sector. Although knowledge entrepreneurs have a sense of independence and freedom in their daily lives, their incomes are insecure (Lane, 2011: 13–23). They exist like operators of small coastal fishing boats off northern or western Norway. They sit alone in their little boats with their insecure incomes, but none the less they feel that they are leading free and independent lives (Johannessen, 1979). Rates of pay for knowledge entrepreneurs vary, but in general they will earn less than they would have done as permanent employees of the same organizations. Example of knowledge entrepreneurs include IT experts and software engineers. These people tend to work for large organizations on six-month contracts that can be terminated at just a few weeks' notice.

We term the fourth type **vagabond workers**. These workers may be migrants and people with disabilities. They are skilled and educated and differ from 'the working poor'. On the whole, the vagabond workers are satisfied with their working life, because their part-time jobs are better than what they had before. Migrants are often happy to be given the opportunity to get a foothold in their new country; for instance, an engineer from Syria who gets a taxi-driving job, the nurse from Iran who works the nightshift at a hotel or the lawyer who gets a short-term job at a slaughterhouse. In this way, part-time contracts can provide migrants with a qualitatively better life. As mentioned, this type also includes people with various disabilities who previously had no work experience but who can now do a meaningful job, although their income might be low; for instance, someone who is visually impaired working in a call centre, and so on.

The four categories of the precariat have in common that their jobs are temporary and insecure, and they are under pressure with regard to rates of pay and employment rights. They also feel alienated.[7] Quite simply, they feel that their future not only is insecure, but has also been destroyed. The precariat also fear moving down the social ladder to the working poor.

The precariat is not yet a class with a shared ideology. Rather it is made up of isolated individuals who sit on the side-lines of society peering into a world populated by successful people, by the salaried éite – a world where people can plan their futures. This successful élite envisages this new class encroaching on to their manicured lawns, and accordingly they remain obedient to the government in accordance with the principle of protecting the future.[8]

All members of the precariat struggle to obtain steady full-time work. They also work long hours unpaid to show keenness to the employer, with the hope of being preferred if a full-time permanent job becomes available (which it rarely does). Speaking metaphorically, we might say it is easier for a member of the precariat to win the lottery than to obtain a secure, well-paid, full-time job with good prospects. In addition, most members of the precariat[9] lack a sense of solidarity with others in the precariat, the trade union movement or a political party. They feel themselves to be excluded by most established institutions. According to Standing, their basic attitude is 'fuck politics'.[10] Members of the precariat do not see themselves as a social class. They have no collective aims, but simply struggle to make ends meet. It is only when they gain class consciousness as a separate social class that they will come to change the social system (Standing, 2014a: 1–4).

The description above has been developed into a typology, which is shown in Figure 1.2.

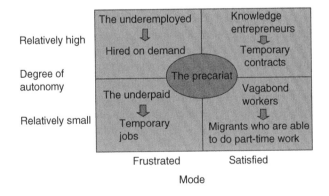

Figure 1.2 A typology of the precariat.

The underemployed

The underemployed go in and out of temporary jobs, and their rights in the labour market are very insecure. They are unable to find jobs that match their education, resulting in existential insecurity (Coates & Morrison, 2016: 134–167). Their broken dreams make them frustrated, angry and at times aggressive. In this frustration lies rebellion, according to Standing (2014a: vii).

Today the proportion of young people with higher education is much greater than in the past. Despite this, Trot (2015: 25–26) says that young people cannot expect to find a job that matches their education. They also have difficulty finding a job they think is meaningful (Coates & Morrison, 2016: 116–134). If and when they get a job, it's often based on a temporary contract and poorly paid.[11]

It seems to be the case that it is the relatively highly educated, rather than those with little education, who experience the greatest uncertainty in finding a job and job security (Armano & Murgia, 2015: 106). For instance, 40 per cent of the graduates in Spain are in poorly paid jobs one year after graduating (Standing, 2014a: 67). The new generation of European university graduates have not been able to realize the future they had envisioned at the outset of their studies (Mason, 2012: 71). They have also taken out loans which they had planned to pay back when finding a job after graduating; this proves difficult when their present income is much lower than they had planned for (Standing, 2014a: 68). This frustration easily leads to anger and rebellion against the establishment (Mason, 2012: 71–80), i.e. the political, economic, intellectual and cultural élite. These indebted students on low incomes also belong to the emerging group of debt-laden home owners. One of the consequences of the situation described is the obedient and disciplined worker hired on a part-time basis and on contract (Lazzarato, 2012: 7).

You're free as long as you can pay your debts, writes Lazzarato (2012: 31). Thus, the underemployed are willing to do any jobs that are available (Coates & Morrison, 2016: 187–217). Those who are highly educated are also willing to do non-paying jobs, so they can get a 'foot inside the door' of large companies – for instance, by means of non-paid or poorly paid 'internships' (Perlin, 2011: 36). These young people had been promised that when they graduated their dreams would be realized (Ainley, 2016: 1–3). In other words, they have been grossly misled; one might even say that a whole generation has been deceived, says Ainley (2016). If and when these young people are given contracts, they are often of only a few months' duration. When their contract runs out, they have to go back to the unemployment office (Armano & Murgia, 2015: 102).

These highly educated young people see their expectations shattered. Although their contracts may give them a high degree of autonomy, their future income is uncertain. Consequently, one might characterize this autonomy as 'fake autonomy' (Armano & Murgia, 2015: 106). This may be explained by the fact that these workers have limited access to welfare benefits, because these benefits are often dependent on being permanently employed.

The underpaid

Every country in the world has its underpaid workers. In the USA, many of the underpaid can be found in the Rust Belt. Historically, these workers can trace their roots back to the days of the New Deal. The lives of these workers have become insecure through work flexibilization, which is a direct consequence of globalization. The underpaid in the American Rust Belt have been unable to compete with the lower wages of Chinese and Mexican workers. Consequently, jobs in the Rust Belt have disappeared or become insecure. At the same time, the power of the unions has been diminished (Varga, 2015: 46). Similar developments have also been taking place in all the other industrialized countries from the 1970s onwards.

Through globalization, the underpaid have joined the ranks of the precariat. They feel betrayed by the political and financial élite. They are desperate and angry, but have nobody else to vent their frustration and anger on than the élite, who have warmly expounded on the benefits of globalization, free trade agreements, and the free flow of capital and labour. Among others, this concerns workers in the American Rust Belt, Wales, Greece, Spain, Italy, France and other countries (Abrahamson, 2004). The underpaid can also be found in the service sector in big cities (Abrahamson, 2004: 49); their wages have been forced down in the competitive world of globalization. These workers are often immigrants or domestic migrants who take poorly paid jobs. In the EU, social dumping has greatly contributed to swelling the ranks of the underpaid.

The knowledge entrepreneurs

The third type in our precariat typology is the knowledge entrepreneurs. These are people with a higher education, but who cannot get or do not wish for permanent employment (Ikonen, 2015: 84). They belong to the so-called 'self-employed society' (Ainley, 2016: 38). They often have short-term contracts, making their conditions of employment temporary and uncertain (Du Gay & Morgan, 2004). They are freelancers who are independent and work whenever they want or need to. As a rule they don't belong to a trade union. In the USA alone, this group of workers constitutes as many as 54 million people.[12] There are many websites that cater to the employment needs of freelancers, such as Field Nation, Upwork, HourlyNerd, Toptal, Work Market and PwC Talent Exchange, to name just a few.[13]

Many of the knowledge entrepreneurs can be found in big cities (Abrahamson, 2004: 49), where they often operate as 'the company of one' (Lane, 2011). As a rule, they are often employed on temporary and insecure contracts. Their dreams are often linked to becoming innovation workers and knowledge workers, and hopefully thus becoming one of the salaried élite (Standing, 2014b: 14). Becoming a knowledge worker or innovation worker is the knowledge entrepreneur's opportunity for upward social mobility.

On the personal level, the uncertainty of contract work requires a great deal of stamina and self-discipline (Ikonen, 2015: 83–90). The hypothesis is that the more insecure and less predictable the future, the more people will aim to become knowledge entrepreneurs because they can thus take responsibility for their own future by establishing businesses. However, only a few can make a living out of working as a knowledge entrepreneur. Therefore, they alternate between their own businesses and temporary contract jobs in large companies (Ikonen, 2015: 83). For some, the solution is to move to the big cities because the opportunities for temporary contracts are better there (Ikonen, 2015: 84–85). Domestic migration, however, is not an option for everybody (Tolonen, 2005). This may be partly explained by the fact that, when life is uncertain and insecure, having a local home-base reinforces one's identity and security (Bolanski & Chiapello, 2017).

The knowledge entrepreneur has to deal with areas of responsibility that were formerly the responsibility of the employer, such as working hours, taxes, social security costs, responsibility for job security and so on. The point being made here is that knowledge entrepreneurs do not necessarily have the freedom normally associated with entrepreneurs. This is where the term 'entreployee' (Pongratz & Voss, 2003) may be justified. The knowledge entrepreneur is both an entrepreneur and an employee (Pongratz & Voss, 2003: 6–8).

The vagabond workers

The vagabond workers are relatively well educated, but they often have a disability or are migrants. They take on low-paid jobs, but are nevertheless satisfied because the alternative is so much worse (Banki, 2015: 66).

The vagabond workers distinguish themselves from the working poor with their higher level of education. However, there are also many migrants among the working poor with a low level of education.

The work situation of the vagabond workers is characterized by a very high level of uncertainty. They are often in a waiting position. They are waiting for new contracts, waiting to 'advance' to becoming knowledge entrepreneurs and waiting for their children to join the salaried elite. However, the opportunities for upward social mobility are very low for this group (Standing, 2014b: 166).

After World War II, wages and wage increases constituted the strongest "contract" between employers and employees. This led to stable conditions and a working class that accepted flexibility of employment conditions and global competition, because expectations of better pay could always counterbalance the disadvantages of work flexibilization (Rothkopf, 2009, 2012). Most political parties in Europe and the USA have accepted and worked for this social employee contract, thus reinforcing this development, which has also been supported by the middle class.

All members of today's precariat are motivated by the dream of joining the salaried élite (Coates & Morrison, 2016: 23–59). The salaried élite are made up of people with secure, highly paid, permanent jobs. They continue to believe in the social contract between employer and employee. However, our point is simply that the salaried élite will also be crushed and decimated by the mill-stones of globalization (Standing, 2014b: 14–28).

The vagabond workers are low paid and often hired on contracts that favour the employer to the disadvantage of the worker. These contracts, which Standing (2014b: 165) calls 'zero-hour contracts', provide extremely high flexibility of the work situation for employers. In addition, the vagabond workers are often excluded from the social benefits that the salaried elite, the knowledge entrepreneurs and the underemployed have established.

Sub-conclusion

The sub-research question we have examined in this section is: How does the precariat constitute an aspect of the Fourth Industrial Revolution?

After World War II and up to today we have witnessed a development that may be described thus: from jobs without education, to education without jobs. Previously, education provided a gateway to the middle class, whereas the situation today suggests something different. This situation may be summarized in the following statement: 'Globalisation is making the middle class of the "old" industrialised nations poor, whereas in the world's emerging industrialised nations, we are witnessing the opposite trend – the middle class is growing strongly.'

Among the challenges facing those with higher education today, robotization has taken over many traditional work operations. This development is increasing in strength, and is affecting most middle-class jobs. This has had a negative effect on the number of middle-class jobs available, and is contributing to an erosion of the middle class.

Not only is the precariat experiencing uncertainty about their employment situation, but there is also much to suggest they are also experiencing existential uncertainty. This may be related to the following type of question: 'What is the point of a higher education when we meet insurmountable difficulties in getting a job that matches our education?' Thus, the precariat is characterized by both economic and social deterioration.

The precariat is also subjected to a special form of blackmail: either they accept an insecure and poorly paid job, or they end up unemployed without any particular form of economic security network. This development leads to, on the one hand, subordination and obedience (which is perceived as a weakening of their autonomy), and, on the other, to a feeling of frustration and anger concerning one's life situation.

The wages levels of the precariat are constantly under pressure. New migrants and other unemployed workers compete for the same jobs and push wages down further. In addition, the precariat is put under pressure by workers in low-cost countries.

Among other things, the growth of the precariat may be seen as a result of the increasing flexibilization of the labour market and the new global division of labour. In this context, the flexibilization of the labour market means that it is easier for an employer to terminate an employee.

There is a vague line between temporary employment contracts and temporary entrepreneurial income. This vague line also means that most people do not manage to come to grips with the new uncertainty that is developing in the workplace. One explanation for this lack of understanding of the workplace's uncertainty may be linked to the identity of the entrepreneur. The entrepreneur perceives him- or herself largely as the author of his or her own success, and thus does not regard the new working conditions as the reason for his or her relatively low income.

The working poor

Description

The working poor can be found in every country in the world today. They work in factories, on farms and in the service industry, such as the hotel industry and other sectors. These workers are largely 'invisible'. They can be illegal immigrants or unskilled workers who have lost their jobs and do part-time jobs for several employers.

The working poor are invisible in the sense that they are rarely included in official statistics. They balance on the edge of poverty, but manage to keep their heads above water, often because they have several jobs. There are many who need these part-time jobs, which often only amount to two or three hours per day. These mini-jobs are in demand and therefore competition forces wages down further. The working poor also compete with imported goods and services from low-cost countries in Asia and Africa, which pushes wages further down. The working poor thus struggle against the feeling of hopelessness, and are forced to take bad jobs at bad wages. In terms of economic survival, they are constantly moving towards the bottom and almost falling into poverty. The working poor also constitute the future labour reserve, and they are willing to do any job for low wages so as not to sink deeper into the swamp of poverty. Shipler (2005) describes these people's lives in the USA. However, they may also be found to the same extent in Europe (Grain et al., 2016).

These workers sometimes work in full-time jobs for poor pay. In addition, they may have one or more part-time jobs just to scrape by (Allen, 2004: 216). They are 'forced to work any job no matter how dirty, embarrassing or dangerous, in fear of losing the benefits' (Ainley, 2014: 3).[14]

The working poor are mainly migrants with poor education, but many of them are nationals. For example, in India 90 per cent of all workers are hired on informal contracts in poorly paid jobs.[15]

The working poor also struggle with the fact that many of them do not have citizenship in the country where they work, only a residential permit. This excludes them from many of the democratic processes, and their rights are often severely limited. They are also faced with the prospect of having to leave the country in which they live and work. Consequently, they often try to become 'invisible' by ducking under the radar of the public authorities.

As a result of their low income, these migrant workers end up living in ghetto-like areas where rents are very low. Banki (2015: 68–69) also refers to instances of these workers in Thailand, where poorly paid Burmese migrants may be found in certain geographical areas. Altogether, there are about two million Burmese migrants living in Thailand (Banki, 2015: 72). Arnold (2005: 319–340) also shows how these Burmese workers live under very poor conditions. He makes the point that the workers keep the costs down for the global companies operating in these areas.

In other countries, such as Russia, many factory workers are so poorly paid that they are unable to cope with the wages they receive (Morris, 2012). In the post-Soviet period, worker solidarity has been greatly weakened, contributing to the deterioration of wage levels (Morris, 2012).

The working poor can be found doing the lowest-paid jobs in the service industry, such as cleaning jobs in hotels. We also find the working poor doing jobs in the restaurant industry at the bottom of the pay scale. With the rapid growth of robot technology, it is most probable that many of these jobs will also become redundant, and that pay will be further reduced for those remaining (Ross, 2016: 39–40).

We have developed a framework to illustrate the working poor (Figure 1.3). The framework also shows how we have organized this sub-chapter.

Analysis and discussion

In this section, we discuss the elements in the above framework.

Drivers towards the bottom

The emergence of the working poor in Europe may in part be traced back to the Hartz reforms in Germany. The Hartz reforms were a set of recommendations on the reform of the German labour market submitted in 2002 by a committee led by Peter Hartz (hence the name of the reforms). The recommended changes were

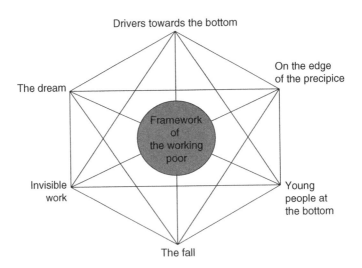

Figure 1.3 A framework for the description of the 'the working poor'.

gradually phased in up until 2010 as part of German labour market policy. The committee proposed ten innovation modules to streamline and increase the flexibility of working life. The various innovation modules were introduced as Hartz I to Hartz IV. In particular, Hartz II led to so-called mini-jobs[16] becoming a part of German working life. The Hartz reforms also resulted in many new job centres being established around the country. The aim of these was to get more workers to take the so-called mini-jobs.

Hartz IV was implemented in 2005. This largely concerned the coordination of social welfare benefits. This resulted in a lower level of social welfare support overall, on average about 391 euros per month in 2013. In addition, unemployed workers were obliged to take any job offered to them, including the mini-jobs.[17] If the unemployed person did not accept the mini-job offered, they lost their 391 euros in welfare support. However, before an unemployed worker could receive any social welfare benefits, they had to document that they had used up all their savings first. When the unemployed worker takes up a mini-job, his or her social welfare benefit is withdrawn.[18] This led to minimum wages in Germany spiralling downwards. Consequently, wages in general were pushed down and there were more people having to do several jobs in order to support themselves and their families. These developments help partly explain the emergence of the working poor in Germany. Although unemployment has fallen sharply in Germany after the introduction of the Hartz reforms, there has also been a very high increase in the number of the working poor during the same period.[19]

It is a common assumption that we identify with our work. Furthermore, the assumption is that we create our identity through our work (Reich, 2015: 133). However, this assumption is challenged in the case of the working poor and parts of the precariat, especially the underemployed and the underpaid. Work does not contribute to the identity of the aforementioned groups. It is the dream of a better future that creates their identity. When both parents have several mini-jobs, and yet barely manage to keep the family away from poverty, they do not see work as a place where they can realize themselves. They work only to keep the wolf from the door. In deep contrast, there is an ever-increasing number of rich people: the very rich (Dorling, 2015). Some of these very rich do not work, but live off their wealth. Others work, but have an incredibly high income compared with the working poor (McGill, 2016).

In the past, poverty has usually been linked to unemployed and sick people. In many countries, these groups get food and shelter from charities. Nowadays, there is an increasing tendency for the poor to include even those who work hard because they are unable to support themselves on the small income they receive. These poor people are not lazy. They are not work-shy. They often have more than one job, but still remain poor (Grain et al., 2016).

There are many reasons for this trend. One is that global neoliberal ideology exploits competition between workers, forcing wages down. Political apathy is a second reason. The low numbers of trade union membership is a third reason. Robotization of working life is a fourth reason. Lack of education is a fifth reason.

In 2013, there were 47 million poor people in the USA. This means that every seventh American (about 14 per cent) lives in poverty (Reich, 2015: 134). Reich writes that, between 2010 and 2013, wages for the 20 per cent lowest paid in the USA fell by 8 per cent. Of those who worked more than a normal work-day, yet were under the government-defined poverty line, half received food handouts from various charities (Reich, 2015: 134).

How could so many workers over such a short period of time suddenly be worth so little in terms of wages? The answer is that globalization increased competition – pushing down wages. Companies wished to reduce costs, so they outsourced to low-cost countries. Company operations were moved in part or in their entirety to low-cost countries. For instance, American companies were moved to Mexico, German companies were moved to Poland and Romania, and labour-intensive companies in the west were moved to China and India. The most recent developments show a relocation of jobs from China to Bangladesh and Myanmar. The result of the above examples is that competition forces down wage levels. This has also led to unemployment, uncertainty and an increase in the number of working poor.

In addition to the above developments, automation, digitization, artificial intelligence and robotization have affected the entire labour market. One of the consequences is that many middle-class work operations have been taken over by robots with artificial intelligence, thus pushing middle-class workers into lower-paid service jobs (Reich, 2015: 134). Thus, several factors are forcing down wages, resulting in the wages of the working poor coming under pressure.

The number of low-paid workers belonging to a trade union in the USA is very low. This applies to hotel workers, restaurant workers, workers in retail sales and fast-food chains, and so on (Reich, 2015: 134–135). In the Nordic countries, minimum wages and the number of workers belonging to a trade union are higher than in the USA, and in a number of countries in southern Europe such as Spain, Greece and Italy (Gratton, 2011: 105–133). This means that we have not yet seen a large growth of the working poor in the Nordic region.

On the edge of the precipice

It's not a question of the working poor lacking ambition, commitment, dreams or the desire to work. It is rather that they are paid too little for the work they actually do, so they are unable to support themselves and their families. In the first decades after World War II (1945–1990), a poor person in the USA had approximately a 50 per cent chance of climbing up the social ladder to the middle class. Today, in stark contrast, it is highly probable that a poor person will remain poor (Reich, 2015: 139).

The new poor, the working poor, are also recruited from the many who dropped out of secondary school, i.e. they are unskilled. In the past, they could find jobs in industry, agriculture, the service sector, transport, the roadworks industry, the construction industry, on ships, and so on. Today, these avenues of employment are largely closed to these people because such jobs require vocational training. In addition, many of the jobs are now automated and taken over by various types of robots. The unskilled workers can now find jobs in the retail industry, fast food chains, and other places where wages and the level of trade union membership are low. But even in these sectors, robotization and artificial intelligence have taken over a number of work operations previously performed by unskilled workers.

There is a low awareness among the working poor concerning the benefit of joining a trade union to ensure higher pay (Shipler, 2005), partly because they come from poorly educated families (Grain et al., 2016). The young working poor even risk competing with their parents and grandparents for the same jobs. Even though their parents had a poor education, they could at least find jobs in industry, such as the car industry in Detroit. The assembly line technology, which was the distinctive feature of Fordism and industrialization, has now spread throughout the world. The 'global assembly line' today is located in various regions according to a logic of costs, quality, competence and innovation. The factory jobs in Detroit's automotive industry disappeared to the low-cost countries. Working in the retail trade for poor pay was an option for those who could no longer find a job in the automotive industry. However, former factory workers might find themselves competing with their own sons or daughters for the same poor pay (Ainley, 2016).

In the UK, Germany, France, Belgium, Spain, Greece, Italy and other western European countries, the same trend, as described above in the USA, is taking place, i.e. the emergence of the new poor underclass, the working poor (Gratton, 2011: 105–133). When steel production moved from European countries such as Germany, France and Belgium to China and other low-cost countries, many former industrial workers were made redundant. Other jobs at the same wage level were hard to find. After a period of time, when welfare support was lost, these unskilled workers joined the ranks of the working poor. Simultaneous with this trend, youth unemployment has increased in most EU countries (Armano & Murgia, 2015: 102–117). Many young people seeking work have tried their luck in other EU countries and, although some have been successful, most have joined the working poor (Banki, 2015: 66–79).

Today, a large part of the younger generation are having to struggle with economic exclusion. Their fathers and mothers lost their jobs in the factories and failed to find similar jobs. Their grandparents have moved back 'home', because pension funds were decimated during the last major economic crisis which started in the autumn of 2007 (Reich, 2015: 139–141). Fear of the future, fear of the unknown and the shame of failing to meet the challenges posed by the global economy characterize parts of the working poor (Gratton, 2011: 110).

At the same time as this psychological description becomes a reality, another psychological factor is on the rise. It is becoming ever more important to stand out from the crowd. Narcissistic self-presentation is becoming part of contemporary youth culture. The reason for this is straightforward. Young people believe this gives them the best opportunity to stand out from the crowd and be in a position to secure a better future (Gratton, 2011: 111). How have so many ended up on the edge of the precipice – staring down into the abyss of poverty?

The neoliberal global capitalism that started in the late 1970s must take a significant part of the blame for the fact that many young people today believe they may suffer poverty in the future (Atkinson, 2010). Poverty is spreading like an epidemic, not only in poor countries, but in the heart of the rich industrial nations. This trend has led to the claim that neoliberal globalization ideology is making the middle class poor. One could paraphrase this and say that globalization makes rich nations poorer and poor nations richer. Bubbles and economic crises are eroding the savings of millions of people. It's not only those who dropped out of school who end up joining the working poor, but also the unskilled industrial workers, the skilled industrial workers and craftsmen, because robotization forces even more workers into unemployment. At the same time, the middle class are being pushed into poverty because artificial intelligence is taking over many of the typical middle-class work functions. The retirees who lost their savings due to economic crises have also joined the army of the poor.

Young people at the bottom

At the bottom of the labour market we find the young people who dropped out of school. These young people never completed a trade education, such as carpentry, electrical engineering, plumbing, and so on. They wash cars, do part-time jobs in shops when there is demand, sell burgers in MacDonald's and other fast food chains. They help you find what you want in the big store chains and wash your windows. They often live at home, even though their peers have long since established a family (Shipler, 2005).

Some of them may manage to climb out of this economic hole; however, few will achieve this. It is those with talent and strong motivation to lift themselves out of poverty who will move up the social ladder. But, most of these young people will remain in poverty the rest of their lives.

It is not the alcoholic, the drug addict or the lazy person we are talking about here. The young people who have joined the working poor do the best they can. Their parents did the best they could too. Both groups are held down in poverty by a system that is served by having workers who are willing to work for a pittance. They do not try to change the structures that hold them where they are (Gratton, 2011). These are the apathetic young who are tired of political promises and empty promises. They don't trust politicians who are interested only in improving their own lot, and that of their children.

The fall

Young people who have become the working poor, their parents and their grandparents are not only poor, but also socially excluded from participating in the wealth they see around them (Chomsky, 2016a, 2016b). The sense of social exclusion is the sense of having been 'left behind', of having been left out in the forest to die. The Ancient Greeks used social exclusion to punish their political opponents. Such a punishment is so extreme that death may seem a better alternative, as shown by the example of Socrates. Socrates chose to drink a glass of poison rather than be banished. The absence of contact with others, with the society one is part of, is the punishment borne by the poor. Punishment for what? They are being punished for not living up to society's expectations regarding 'education, education, education' (Wakeling & Savage, 2015). Those who do succeed in becoming educated will, however, still find it difficult in the Fourth Industrial Revolution to secure jobs that correspond to their level of education (Wakeling & Savage, 2015). The few people who manage to educate themselves out of the working poor will end up in the precariat (Standing, 2014a).

The working poor live in their own residential areas. They shop in their own low-price stores. However, they are very aware of this separation from the rest of society (Monbiot, 2016: 9). Social exclusion is a form of loneliness that affects all age groups, but possibly it is greatest among the young working poor. Monbiot (2016: 10) writes: 'Ebola is unlikely ever to kill as many people as the disease of loneliness.' It is the social isolation and exclusion from the community, 'the disease of loneliness', that affects many around the world. We cannot manage on our own. That is why poor young people and other poor people seek to form a community together. However, this also reinforces the feeling of being excluded from the wealth of the gluttonous society. In addition, this community at the bottom of society reinforces social imbalances and reproduces poverty. The speed of the social collapse we see in the case of the precariat and the working poor can be compared with the rapidity of the spread of innovations. Those on the lowest rung of the social ladder who can be regarded as part of the working poor no longer have the dream of educating themselves for a trade or profession to support themselves in the future. Their dream is essentially linked to becoming rich and famous (Monbiot, 2016: 10). But, this will remain only a dream. Their lives are visible to others only when they take part in movements that will change the structures that hold them down. They will remain invisible until they begin to claim more of society's economic surplus.

Invisible work

Much of the cotton that clothes are made from is picked by underpaid workers in poor countries. The health of these farm workers is also often affected by the poison that is sprayed on the fields to ensure maximum profits from the cotton plantations (Chomsky, 2012, 2016a, 2016b). After the cotton is classified and packed it is sent to countries such as Bangladesh, where new invisible underpaid workers produce clothes from the raw cotton. Thus, people don't 'see' these workers when they buy suits or dresses in western stores. The clothes are labelled, given a brand name – and it is the quality and price that are in focus. The price is the most essential factor. The price is kept low because the wages of the workers who make the clothes are extremely low. These workers in the global economy are the invisible poor workers (Hochschild, 2016: xi). The global production chain makes the poverty invisible for those who contribute to pushing prices further down when they buy products such as shoes or dresses.

In the industrialized world that largely buys these cheap clothes, many workers who previously worked in the domestic textile factories have been made redundant. The models who display the clothes such as dresses, suits, shoes, however, match the ideas the buyers have about the aesthetic (Stewart, 2016: 130–148). This presentation and advertising of the clothes make the workers behind these clothes even more invisible. A similar global production chain exists for most industries, including the food industry (Otis & Zhao, 2016: 148–169).

It is not only in the cotton and clothing industry that we find the invisible poor workers. Many businesses have seen the benefits of sending some of their operations to low-cost countries, for example to Bangalore in India. This may be part of their financial, informational, information technology (IT), sales or human resources (HR) operations. In those countries where operations are exported to low-cost countries, the pressure to reduce wages is also increased. The reason is straightforward. Global competition pushes down wages throughout the whole of the global production chain. This problem is very widespread. More than 50 per cent of all the Fortune 500 companies have outsourced much of the work to low-cost countries that they previously performed domestically (Poster, 2016: 87–113). The invisible workers are one of the factors that impact the future workplaces in the industrialized countries.

What is not shown when the poor workers in the global value chain are made invisible? What is hidden is, among other things, the structural constraints. Coercion and oppression need not be linked to personal relationships. Coercion and oppression, and in part violence, can be found in the structures created by the global value chain. However, one cannot mobilize anger and aggression against structures. Therefore, we often see frustration taking irrational directions, and leading to arbitrary violence and other social manifestations that seem completely irrational.

The prices of the goods we buy in the west often do not reflect the work effort that produced them. Prices reflect only how far down wages can be pushed to increase profits. Yet 50 years ago we could see the whole value chain in our local towns and villages in the factories and on the farms. During this period, trade unions were more effective in negotiating pay conditions whereas today this has become very difficult globally. Today, we are buyers of goods produced by poor workers in countries such as Bangladesh. We have become more concerned about the price of the goods than the conditions the workers who produce the goods work under. In the past, we could talk to the boss at the factory and respond through a trade union. Today, the workers in Bangladesh are unable to talk to, for instance, the boss in Wal-Mart or other chains. They notice only that their wages are reduced or when they lose their jobs because production has moved somewhere else, such as Mozambique, Zaire, Angola, Myanmar, or other low-cost countries. The global value chain makes what was once visible to everyone in the factories into invisible work in, for example countries like Bangladesh and Myanmar.

The dream

All the young people that Shipler (2005: 231–235) talked to had a desire to continue their studies by going to college, because they knew it was the only way to get out of poverty. Many of their parents were unemployed, so they knew what poverty was in practice.

Most of their parents did not have a trade. Sixty per cent of the children Shipler interviewed wanted to be lawyers so they could help people. The ambitions and dreams of these teenagers (aged 12–14 years) were clearly evident. When asked where they thought they would be in 10 years, almost all of them answered that they saw themselves as doctors, lawyers, dentists, archaeologists, and so on. The vision of the future was bright and positive for them. However, the reality 10 years after they were first asked about their dreams was something quite different. Ten years later, most of them are now are poor young people without educational qualifications or work (Shipler, 2005: 233–242). Everything is possible until one's dreams are crushed in the meeting with reality.

The politicians have expressed a vision that all young people should get an education so that they can cope with the emerging economy. The new economy, no matter what we call it, will be characterized by the use of robots, informatization, digitization and computerization of work. In addition, value creation will be spread over the globe.

If nations are to succeed in such a situation, they must develop a focused strategy. China developed such a focused strategy in the late 1980s[20] for foreign investment in China. Bangalore in India has also developed such a strategy. They aimed to become world leaders in the software industry. However, in the process of transformation that we are now in, it would not be the right strategy to depend on the market for domestic development. We have seen the consequences of such a neoliberalist strategy in Wales and in West Virginia (the Rust Belt in the USA). The results are disappointing. Unemployment is high, pay levels poor and the level of education also poor (Ross, 2016: 42–43).

Sub-conclusion

The question we have investigated in this section is: 'How do the working poor constitute an aspect of the Fourth Industrial Revolution?' The short answer is: those who drop out of school in the west enter the ranks of the working poor. These people will be socialized into poverty. Through their defeats and failures at school, they have learned to become losers, the future working poor.

The working poor perform work that is essential for others so they can enjoy their lives and live in abundance. Social mobility is threatened by these new structures. The working poor are structurally locked into a poor existence, without much opportunity to climb up the social ladder from their first job and upwards in the wages hierarchy.

Unemployment statistics are no longer as relevant as they were in the past. Unemployment may be low, but the working poor can barely live off their wages. The trends of more part-time jobs, mini-jobs and the flexibility of working life have created a new underclass below the precariat. They have jobs and are thus not included in unemployment statistics, but find it hard to get by despite having more than one job.

The more detailed answer to the question we have examined in the section is linked to the shifting of economic and social tectonic plates. The factors that will change the workplace of the future are automation, informatization, digitization, robots and informats. This shifting of economic tectonic plates will destroy the old economic and social continent, and create a new continent with completely new social structures.

This development creates new jobs in the industrialized world, even though the entrance fee in terms of expertise is high. Behind these new jobs, however, is a global value chain where invisible workers make this possible. The new continent consists of robots that perform work functions that were previously carried out by many workers. Productivity increases with the new technology. This applies not only to industry. For instance, in hospitals, robots are being developed for diagnosis, medication and operations, and to function as nursing assistants and nurses. Some businesses have developed receptionists in the form of holograms connected to a digital system. This development, however, demands more engineers in the software industry, which places the jobs of nurses and nursing assistants in the risk zone.

In the service industry, which employs millions of people in the west, we find hotel receptionists, restaurant workers, childcare workers, home helpers, cleaning workers, and so on. These workers are meeting strong competition for their jobs on many fronts, such as from immigrants and unemployed people. Consequently, wages are squeezed and working conditions worsened. This constitutes part of the structures that are creating the working poor.

The globalization of the workforce has led to global competition forcing down wages. When wages are forced down, profits increase for the few. This means that the numbers of the poor will increase, whereas the few become richer and richer. We will experience the economy being divided into four parts: first, the super-rich, also referred to as the 1 per cent class; second, the salaried élite consisting of the knowledge workers and innovation workers; third, the precariat, who will probably constitute the largest part of the workforce; and, finally, we have the working poor. There is much to suggest that those receiving welfare support will be forced into mini-jobs, as a consequence of measures such as the German Hartz reforms mentioned above. In this way, the working poor will increase in number.

The cocktail of lower pay, higher unemployment, rising profits and more innovations will most likely lead to continual stock market bubbles and economic crises, both large and small. These crises will spread extremely quickly due to new technology. This will be particularly true of the new robotic systems that will control financial transactions. The rate at which these crises will spread will lead to instability and insecurity for everyone, but it is the working poor who will suffer poverty, whereas the wealthy will merely suffer limited adversity.

It is not new technology that causes millions of workers to lose their jobs and end up in the ranks of the working poor. It is solely an intentional political act that is the cause of this development. Robotization could, if desired, have resulted in increased productivity and value creation being shared by more people. In this way, poverty could have been abolished and working hours reduced. Many people could have had a better life with robots, informats, digitization and informatization. What is happening now is that we are creating a global underclass: the working poor. It is possible that a cocktail of frustrated groups within the precariat and the working poor will contain sufficient explosive force to change political structures in most societies.

The innovation worker and the knowledge worker

Description

Peter Drucker (1999a, 1999b) describes knowledge workers as those who use their intellectual abilities to perform their work. Florida (2002) takes this a step further and describes knowledge workers as the creative and innovative class. Lessard and Baldwin (2000) take a different perspective and call knowledge workers 'net slaves' who are victims of the new technology. Sennett (2006) regards knowledge workers as 'the new spirit of capitalism'. Knowledge workers are thus difficult to define, and they constitute a multi-faceted group. What is common to this group is that they develop, transfer and work with symbols. In essence, knowledge workers are either employees in organizations or else they perform work activities for organizations in other ways, such as consultancy work or contract work. In some cases, there may be an unclear boundary between knowledge workers and knowledge entrepreneurs. What distinguishes the two groups is that knowledge workers generally have permanent well-paid jobs, whereas knowledge entrepreneurs are often hired on temporary, insecure contracts.

Innovation workers and knowledge workers belong to the salaried élite, the well-paid section of salaried employees. Both innovation workers and knowledge workers adhere to the idea that only a postgraduate education, such as a Master's or PhD, can ensure a good job in the future, i.e. they believe such an education is necessary in order to be successful.

One of the results of globalization is that companies have realized that creativity, expertise and innovation are the new competitive parameters (Case, 2016). Profit relies heavily on businesses being able to bring creativity and innovation to the market (Bleuer et al., 2017; Xie, 2017; Zhao et al., 2017). This is where innovation workers emerge as being the solution to a problem. The problem is that businesses are unable to compete on costs, so therefore they must compete on innovation.

Education in the global economy has become a commodity in line with other commodities. Thus, in the future, the quality, brand and reputation of educational institutions will be given greater emphasis. This will result in an increased emphasis on the ranking of educational institutions – that is to say, students from the best universities will be given more opportunities in their working lives (Savage, 2015: 221–257). Universities are popping up like mushrooms around the world. In China alone there were approximately 300 universities with 20 million students in 2008, and in that year, 6 million students graduated.[21] This only reinforces the tendency towards gradation of educational institutions around the world. The consequences for graduates are obvious. The graduates from the less prestigious universities will have fewer opportunities in the job market, whereas graduates from the top universities will have the best opportunities. Savage (2015: 221) clearly states: 'universities are affecting future careers'.

The time is past when higher education itself opened all the doors for future career opportunities (Savage, 2015: 290–296). First, the length and depth of an education are important. A Master's or PhD is becoming a necessary condition to be being an innovation and knowledge worker. However, this alone is not sufficient. A decisive factor is the reputation, and hence the quality, of the university where one earns one's degree. The élite universities open doors for those who want to be innovation workers and knowledge workers with future dream jobs. These will eventually join the salaried élite, helping to maintain the reproduction of social inequality (Savage, 2015: 222; Wakeling & Savage, 2015a). The mediocre and poor universities provide opportunities for those who will be knowledge entrepreneurs and will thus belong to the precariat.

We have visualized the innovation worker and the knowledge worker in their future roles in Figure 1.4.

Analysis and discussion

In this section we discuss the five elements in the above framework.

Pyjama-workers

Innovation workers who have relatively autonomous working lives are as likely to work in their pyjamas, and from their beds, as in the office (Tapia, 2009). This suggests that flexible working will become more in demand than work–life balance. Innovation workers will be able to manage their own working and leisure time. For an innovation worker, being at work is not the same as being at the office. Being at work means being engaged in a task, and then it is less important whether one is lolling in bed or wandering around the garden in one's pyjamas. It is all about the product – not about clocking in at the office. The industrial logic in the minds of many managers hinders innovation processes, however, because these managers want to control and manage their workforce. It is very likely, however, that this kind of management style will soon be past its sell-by date.

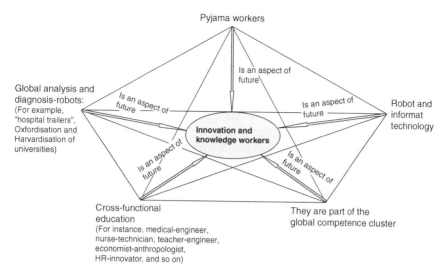

Figure 1.4 A framework for future innovation workers and knowledge workers.

What characterizes the innovation worker is that he or she is extremely connected in social networks. These workers largely belong to the millennium generation, those born between 1977 and 1997. We find them to a large extent in major global businesses such as Deloitte, Cisco, Bell Canada, Jetblue, Google, Apple, NASA, Facebook, Proctor & Gamble, Nike, Lockheed Martin, and so on (Meister & Willyerd, 2010). These people are extremely committed to what they are working on. Their social life is largely their work, and they are what may be termed 'über-connected' (Meister & Willyerd, 2010: 122–124). The businesses where innovation workers work largely use social media to develop their reputation (consumer brand) (Meister & Willyerd, 2010: 123). In the future, it is the reputation of the business that will be a key factor in its success. Therefore, it is crucial how the business is perceived by the outside world. The same goes for the innovation worker. His or her reputation is his or her trademark.

In the global knowledge economy, the office of the innovation worker and the knowledge worker will be wherever they happen to have access to their digital technology. This technology may be embodied in a smart phone, laptop, robot computer, 'holographic machine', nano-technology, etc. (Avent, 2016). He or she can thus work lying in bed in pyjamas, or at a café bar.

As a rule, the innovation worker will want to work at 'third places', not at the location of the actual business, nor at home, but at a third place, such as a holiday cabin, a coffee shop, a hotel, on the train, at the airport, on the beach or on a hiking trip in the Alps, and the like. The pyjama workers work where they are most creative, and this is rarely at a fixed office location from 9 to 5.

It is important to note that, although innovation and knowledge workers are creative and skilled, their success is often linked to the team they work with (Grant, 2014). In the global knowledge economy, this team is spread out across the globe. Consequently, innovation and knowledge workers often work in global competence clusters.

This insight will most probably lead to hiring and problem-solving processes for innovation workers and knowledge workers, veering away from the employment of individuals and towards hiring entire teams. It may also be imagined that teams are used in the innovation process, without actually employing the team. This process may be called 'crowdsourcing', a term introduced by Howe (2006). Specifically, this means that businesses, such as Lego, Procter & Gamble and Boeing use 'the wisdom of crowds' (Surowiecki, 2005) to solve problems. Grant (2014) also found this to be a success factor in his research. The teams may be located in the global space in global competence clusters. Global competence clusters are not geographically located in one place, but are spread over the global social network. They come together when there is a problem that they have special talents to solve. Global competence clusters may be imagined as being activated in response to a specific problem. The problem is then solved by the global competence cluster working in unison. Once the problem has been solved, the specific global competence cluster is dissolved.

A controversial proposal, but certainly a realistic one, is that innovation and knowledge workers will have a preference for electing their own leaders. There are already businesses where the head manager is appointed by the board, whereas the middle managers are elected from and by the employees. Meister and Willyerd (2010: 224) refer to W.L. Goore & Associates, where the head manager allows employees to elect their own middle managers. An important criterion for being elected is for you to have shown that you are a team builder and that you can make the team work effectively. In the example mentioned above, several selection criteria were used and analysed to select the leader. One of the benefits of this approach is reported to be a very low turnover of staff in the business (Meister & Willyerd, 2010: 222–226).

Robot and informat technology

Our assumption is that jobs and careers in the future will be under pressure due to many factors. The two most important factors are probably global competition and new technology.

Global competition will most probably lead to the greater part of jobs being affected. In this context, average wages will be reduced, although productivity will increase radically (Avent, 2016).

Productivity will be greatly increased due to new technology (Abd, 2017; Wilson, 2017). The new technology, consisting of robots, artificial intelligence, informats, nano-computers, analysis and diagnostic machines will take over parts of, and in some cases entire functions and processes of, jobs previously carried out by people (Wilson, 2017; Zhao et al., 2017). This is not a case of 10, 20 or

30 per cent of the jobs, but as high as 50–80 per cent of jobs being taken over by the new technology, such as robots and informats.[22]

The extent of robotization will vary from country to country. Countries that produce robots and sell them on the international market will be able to increase employment. In this context, Ross (2016: 40–41) mentions countries such as South Korea, Japan and Germany. Low-cost countries, such as China and other countries, will be the most vulnerable to this development. However, these countries will also be able to adjust to robotization, but will have to make great efforts to retrain workers, and reform their educational systems to a large extent. If unskilled workers are going to have any hope of getting a job, they will have to retrain to do jobs such as robot operators, robot technicians, robot engineers, robot designers, and so on.

Developments in low-cost countries may be compared with what happened to industrial jobs in the industrialized countries at the end of the twentieth century. One may imagine, for example, that the Chinese leadership could take a dual approach. They continue with their low-cost industry, while focusing on skills development in robot technology (Ross, 2016: 40–41). This may be achieved because the influx of people into urban areas is very high in China and supported by government policies. Urban growth in China has greatly increased in recent decades: in 1950, 13 per cent lived in urban areas, but by 2015 this had risen to 50 per cent. Chinese government policy is to increase this to 70 per cent by 2025.[23] This development will enable competence building, while retaining low costs on labour-intensive industry jobs.

Thus, the Fourth Industrial Revolution is not only making itself visible in the industrialized countries but also in those countries that are in the process of industrialization. If labour wages increase in China, one can imagine that China will subcontract and outsource work to countries such as Bangladesh, Zaire, Angola, Mozambique and other countries in Africa. The beginnings of such a strategy have already started (Gaskarth, 2015; Swider, 2015; Otis et al., 2016). Interesting in this context is the fact that the industrial wage in some Chinese companies (March 2016) is on a par with the industrial wage in southern European countries.[24]

When labour costs increase, while robot technology is becoming cheaper because of mass production, more and more of industrial production and service production will be robotized. This will also force low-cost areas to transform to robot technology, which will open up the opportunity for countries such as China and Germany to educate the workforce, so it can adapt to the great transformation of work and economy.

Robots don't demand pay rises; on the contrary, they get cheaper and cheaper, because they are mass produced. Robots don't go on strike, so they are easy to manage. Robots don't criticize, so they are easy to lead. Robots don't have cultural hang-ups, so they don't generate social and emotional tensions. These are some of the factors behind the great transformation, the transformation of the workforce over a relatively short period through robot technology. This will apply to both industrialized countries and those that are in the process of industrialization.

They are part of a global competence cluster

The security, predictability and safety of permanent jobs in the industrial society will most likely disappear either completely or in part in the Fourth Industrial Revolution (Standing, 2014a; Varga, 2015; Wang, 2015). Innovation and knowledge workers will not need to adhere to a nine-to-five workday – a trend that will eventually spread to the entire workforce (Gratton, 2011: 196). When everything is changing, how can you succeed when you don't know what will be required of you in the future? There are three areas that will determine who succeeds and who fails. The first is their intellectual capital, which concerns the level of education. For the innovation and knowledge workers, this will require a Master's degree or PhD. However, a high level of education is only one necessary condition to achieving success. There are two other sufficient conditions that need to be in place if one is to succeed in the Fourth Industrial Revolution. One factor is social capital, which concerns the social network you are part of and how tightly knit the relationships are that you have in this network. The other factor is one's political capital, i.e. how close the ties are that you have to the person(s) who makes decisions that may affect your future. It is the system composed of these three factors that will be crucial to one's success, when all known work is transformed into something new and unknown (Kessler, 2017).

The rules of the game change when everything is transformed into something new and unknown. Consider companies such as Uber, Google, Instagram, Microsoft, Apple, Cisco, IBM, SunTrust, and so on. These companies behaved strategically, had an extreme customer focus and were capable of extreme change. However, the most important thing about these companies was that they changed the rules of the industry. This is what Christensen terms disruption (Christensen, 2016).

All the job experience we have gained is collapsing. Our future colleagues do not necessarily work at our place of work – they can be scattered around the world in global competence clusters. We do not necessarily have a fixed place of work to go to, but use locations such as coffee shops and the social areas in fitness centres to get in touch with our colleagues in the global competence clusters. Possibly, owners of fitness centres will identify this trend and install small and large office units and canteens.

A large Gallup survey has shown that only 32 per cent of employees are committed to their jobs (Meister & Mulcahy, 2017: 228). This implies that in the future employers should seek those who have talent and also a strong commitment to an idea. We also know with certainty that robots will eliminate bureaucracies and hierarchies. Consequently, when designing workplaces, one should think of functions rather than positions. The innovation worker and the knowledge worker can manage themselves, and do not need intermediaries to set the agenda for their work processes. On the other hand, there will still be requirements regarding which results should be delivered and when.

Workplaces built in the industrial era, with their bureaucracies and hierarchies, will be subjected to transformation. If they are not changed, they will be crushed by the new technology (Arnold, 2005; Bennis et al., 2012). The new organizations and new jobs will most probably be functionally, not hierarchically, organized. The new jobs will be organized in relation to people with talent, with ideas about what makes them feel passionate. Those who are not passionate about an idea will have no place in organizations of the future. The future organization of the workplace will crystallize into an emphasis on the organization's meeting with the customer, the user, the patient, the student, and so on. This design, based on experiences gained from meeting customers and users, will promote a front-line focus and will downplay the past functions of bureaucracy and hierarchy in the industrial society.

Cross-functional education

Robotization not only eliminates bureaucracies and hierarchies, but also changes the professions of knowledge workers. Susskind and Susskind (2015) say this will apply to doctors, nurses, teachers, accountants, architects, priests, consultants, lawyers, and others.

The nature of their work will be completely different from in the pre-robotized society. Robots and artificial intelligence will shatter both the form and the content of the traditional knowledge professions. If such an assumption proves to be correct, the question is: 'What will the content of the knowledge workers' jobs look like when robots take over many of their functions?' The robots referred to here are those driven by artificial intelligence and informats that, in addition to having artificial intelligence, are interconnected globally so they have access to the latest information and research results.

The positive aspect of this development is that industrial robots have created more jobs than they have destroyed.[25] For instance, this applies to welding robots, which require many substructures. The construction of these provides many developmental jobs in the outlying regions of Denmark, says chief economist Allan Lyngsø Madsen of Danish Metal.[26] Madsen's analysis is as follows:

> If automation results in an increase in productivity of 15 percent, then employment will fall by 7 percent within the first three years. However, in the long term, employment will increase because the company will become more competitive and more orders will eventually be placed.[27]

However, the weakness of such an analysis is obvious. If everyone were to do the same as Danish metal, and use more industrial robots, then this will only increase competition overall. The benefits of increased productivity in such a situation will not lead to more sales and more employees, but to increased global competition. This may be likened to standing up from your seat at a football match so as to see the game better. The first few who do this will see the game better, but when everyone does the same then the advantage will be lost. Thus, Madsen's analysis is erroneous in the global competitive economy. Exactly the same reasoning may be used regarding the fact that competition from robots and artificial intelligence eliminates many of the functions that knowledge and innovation workers perform today. Therefore, it is crucial that the education system be reformed to meet these needs before robots make the current education system redundant.

If policy-makers choose to ignore what is happening to knowledge and innovation workers, then their policies will have fatal consequences for the education system, the professions and economic growth (Susskind & Susskind, 2015). It is not hard to understand the new developments that are emerging. The challenge is to get rid of ideas from the industrial society about how to manage and organize work. In addition, it will be a challenge to change many of the educational programmes so that they take into account the ever-increasing use of robots, informats and artificial intelligence.

Changing these mental models will be the hardest of all the tasks. The point is, however, that, if we do not change our ideas from the industrial society, the knowledge society's robots will change our perception of these ideas. Either we must plan our future ourselves, or there are other forces that will make us an obedient tool of their interests. 'Plan or be planned for,' said Ackoff (1989). This applies more than ever today.

Innovation and knowledge workers are experts in their field of study. What should we do with their expertise if a robot with its artificial intelligence coupled with all available knowledge in the global space (informats) can do the same, but with higher quality and safety, and lower costs?

In the near future, users will be able to come into contact with robots that have this expertise at a lower cost and higher performance. This will not necessarily happen overnight, but will be more like a cascade of incremental innovations. Each of these innovations will, like the killer whale, take a small bite from the profession's previous field of operation. Slowly but surely, robots and informats with their artificial intelligence will take over many of the professional tasks that are carried out today, for instance, the tasks of doctors and nurses in the medical profession. In the future, hospitals will become workplaces for engineers just as much as they are for doctors. Doctors and nurses will need a multi-education, i.e. they will possess engineering skills as well as having knowledge of anatomy and diseases. On the other hand, the hospital–engineer will also be educated in anatomy and diseases. Slowly but surely, the lawyer, architect, teacher, economist and HR leader will become assistants of their former assistants, i.e. the robots. In such a scenario, all of these professions will need to include robot technology in their education. Future educational programmes may thus be designed for the medical–engineer, the nurse–technician, the teacher–engineer, the economist–anthropologist and the HR–innovator, to mention just a few.

The future will not resemble the past for innovation and knowledge workers, but will be greatly impacted by the use of robots and informats. Thus, new ways of thinking, new educational programmes, new models and new mental tools will be needed.

Knowledge professions, such as the medical, legal and architect professions, will be greatly affected by the use of robots and informats. The expert has knowledge and experience. Much of this knowledge can be digitized and used in artificial intelligence systems. The same goes for some of the expert's experience. However, not all types of experience can be digitized. We do not yet have the means of digitizing the type of experience known as tacit knowledge. However, in the future this may become possible, using artificial intelligence. This would create a situation where robots and informats would also be able to learn from their experiences. This would pose further challenges for many professions that would have to rethink what is the purpose of their activities.

Companies that had to close down or were bought up for various reasons all have something in common: they ignored what was happening – new developments. They were not future oriented, i.e. they did not think from the future and back to the present. Instead, they thought from the past and then extrapolated the past into the future, i.e. they used history to look forward. The death rate of organizations is high in the knowledge economy. Of the Fortune 500 organizations that have been established since 2000, 51 per cent have closed down (Wang, 2015).

The workplace of knowledge and innovation workers is changing at an unbelievably fast rate. Changes involve where you work, how you work, whom you work with and when you work, and are taking on completely different forms than in the industrial society. Due to robots and informats, future organizations are learning machines that change in step with changes in the outside world. To achieve this, both big and small organizations must organize themselves to be flexible and change quickly. We can say that tomorrow's organizations must be able to change so they can create their own future. The leaders who are able to do this must also encourage their employees to be change agents, and focus on the use of new technology (Bratianu, 2015; Case, 2016).

Apart from pay, knowledge and innovation workers consider flexibility more important than anything else when considering a job offer (Meister & Mulcahy, 2017: 12). To achieve this, there has been a reinvention of goals, results and performance management that has taken another form. The knowledge worker wishes to have full flexibility in relation to where he or she works, when, how and with whom. To achieve this, he or she is willing to enter into contracts concerning what will be delivered over a specific period of time. This may be termed 'performance management', where it is the goals and results that are essential, not where you have your office. This development is already taking place in companies such as Adobe, IBM, General Electric, Microsoft, Accenture and Cisco, to name just a few (Meister & Mulcahy, 2017: 52). Furthermore, the knowledge professions are changing to such an extent that it is becoming more and more common for team intelligence to be crucial, not the individual's performance (Gant, 2014).

Global analysis and diagnosis robots

Traditionally, the patient visits the doctor when he or she doesn't feel well. However, by this time a threshold may already have been exceeded, so that the doctor will need to prescribe medication, with the possibility that this may have side effects. However, if we imagine that everyone has access to a 'diagnosis machine' – let's call this an online informat – then this would change the doctor's work to a great extent. The diagnosis machine will, at a very early stage, be able to provide a report of any disease that is developing and give guidelines on what the individual must and can do to prevent or mitigate the course of the disease. One can further imagine small, mobile hospitals, which we will call 'hospital trailers', filled with technology that can diagnose, medicate, and make simple and complicated interventions. In such a future, the giant hospitals will become a thing of the past. They will become monuments from the industrial age, when size meant success. Today, an important argument is that large hospitals are needed because they provide a meeting place for all the skills that are needed, and that size means it is possible to buy expensive machines. In the near future, these skills will be found in informats. The informats will have more skills than all of the doctors put together in a large super-hospital. If the informats are mass produced, both of the main arguments concerning the need for large hospitals will not be applicable.

If we envisage this kind of future, our gigantic hospitals will be worthless as health-promoting institutions. We use the expression 'hospital trailers' to emphasize that size in the knowledge society is not a recipe for success. The Fourth Industrial Revolution will develop robotized and specialized small units that take account of customers' geographical location rather than the system's need for gigantomania.

The development of small robot systems that can carry out medical functions is already under way. Pacemakers and insulin pumps are two examples. At the University of California in San Francisco, they have their own robot that prints prescriptions without making errors. The normal rate of error among pharmacists is approximately 1 per cent per year, which for the USA amounts to approximately 37 million small and large errors in the handling of prescriptions (Steiner, 2012: 155). Similar robotization is occurring within reading, synthesis, hypothesis development and hypothesis testing of medical research (Susskind & Susskind, 2015: 49).

Using robots and informats in the future, a situation may be imagined in which, when the patient contacts a nursing–technician, it will be possible to carry out most examinations, diagnoses, medications and prescriptions. The medical profession in such an imagined reality will take on completely different roles. Among other things, it would allow the education of doctors to be more orientated towards the development of new knowledge, and not just the application of existing knowledge.

One can also imagine a new type of 'barefoot' doctor – a new profession whose education will provide them with medical, psychological, communications and technological competence. This new profession will function where today's doctors practise. Medical education will in such an imagined scenario have the possibility of becoming more research orientated, by contrast to today's medical education which focuses on research only to a limited extent.

The professions, businesses and organizations that do not adapt to new technology will disappear within the space of a few years. The new technology will be made up of robots, informats and artificial intelligence. In the Fourth Industrial Revolution, people will learn to live side by side with robots and informats that will have a greater logical intelligence and a much larger mega-memory. The first mass production of robots will probably occur in relation to the care of elderly people. This will of necessity come about because elderly people (65+) will soon account for a third of the population. In the future, there will not be enough nurses or resources to take care of all elderly people needing care. Consequently, robots of various types will perform parts of elderly care that are provided today. Japan has the longest life expectancy in the world, and consequently the oldest population. The development of robots has been given priority in a number of Japanese companies, such as Toyota, Honda, Tokai Rubber Industries and AIST. Today, Japan leads the world in the development of robots. This applies to both nursing care robots and industrial robots. The next step we will see in the development of robots, says Ross (2016: 16–18), will be robots that are capable of emotional and social interaction.

However, there are several people who are critical of this development, including MIT's Professor Sherry Turkle. She questions the role of conversation in such a robotization, saying that the transfer of knowledge from the elder to the younger generation will also be jeopardized (Turkle, 2016). There is a possibility that the older generation will be able to transfer their skills to robots and informats. In this way, experience will not only be transferred, but also stored and used. The point that Sherry Turkle overlooks is that conversation and experience transfer can go through robots to the younger generation. With such a development, you will not lose the experience of elderly people, and conversation's art can be learned via an intermediary – the robot who converses with the elderly care patient. As the elderly population in the USA and Europe grows similar to the Japanese, the demand for care-taking robots will explode (Ross, 2016: 19).

The USA, Germany and Japan dominate the market for high-tech medical robots. If we also take into account South Korea and China, we have the five countries that produce and consume most robotic systems (Bond, 2013). The development of these robots is shown in sales statistics. In 2013, 1300 surgical robots were sold. This represented 41 per cent in value of the total sales of industrial robots. In the USA, more than one million people have undergone operations performed by robots, and the number is increasing yearly by 30 per cent (Ross, 2016: 32). This indicates that the use of robots in medical applications may currently be in its infancy but it will soon explode (Xie, 2017). In addition, medical robots will be able to reach places inaccessible to human surgeons, for example at the neuron level in the brain (Goldberg, 2000).

If the developments as described above stay on track, we will see the emergence of 'hospital trailers' sometime between 2023 and 2045.

The development towards 'hospital trailers' will become a reality when two factors are present:

1. When nano robots see the light of day. These will be extremely small but will be able to carry out the diagnosis and medication of various diseases and measure blood pressure, blood sugar, detect the first signs of cancer tumours, as well as identify various threshold values that are important to keep under control.
2. When singularity occurs, i.e. when artificial intelligence becomes equal or better than human logical intelligence (IQ).

It is argued that singularity will occur between 2023 and 2045 due to Moore's law,[28] 'cloud computing', machine learning, 'telerobotics' and 'data analytics' (Ross, 2016: 26–27; Goldberg, 2000).

Sub-conclusion

The question we have investigated in this section is: 'How do knowledge workers constitute an aspect of the Fourth Industrial Revolution?'

Education is only one necessary condition for obtaining a good job. It is also important that one has attended one of the more prestigious universities. However, education is not enough. The sufficient condition is the reputation capital that you have. If you are known to be skilled in idea development, this will become your reputation capital. If you are skilled in executing ideas, then this will become your reputation capital. If you deliver products/services well above the average of the required parameters, then your delivery capacity will be your reputation capital, and so on. In the global economy, education, which university the individual has graduated from, his or her talent and his or her personal reputation are all factors that will secure a job as an innovation and knowledge worker.

When robots and informats take over some of knowledge and innovation workers' functions in organizations and institutions, this will lead to five obvious consequences.

First, *the bureaucracy* will partially disappear because the functions of the bureaucracy will be digitized and taken over by robots.

The second consequence is that *hierarchies* will change their form and character. The bureaucracy was an important component of the organizational hierarchy of the industrial society. When the functions of bureaucracy are taken over by robots, this means that the hierarchy will also be eroded, together with bureaucracy.

The third consequence is that *management roles* will change. There will be more focus on getting teams and projects to work optimally. At the same time, creating the future of the business will become an even more important task for the manager, because the rate of change will increase sharply.

The fourth consequence of pushing down costs and pushing up productivity is *the elimination of the middle class*, or at least it will be virtually decimated. The logic is simple. The middle class is largely linked to control and communication functions in organizations and institutions. It is precisely these functions that robots and informats will take over.

The fifth consequence of the developments described above will be *an increasing inequality in income* between the innovation and knowledge workers, on the one hand, and the precariat and the working poor, on the other. At the same time, we will see a greater income gap between the various sectors in the precariat, which we have described above. In addition to this, those who own capital will receive even higher capital income because of the increase in productivity and the reduction in costs due to global competition. The sum of these developments will be an increasing inequality between wage earners. At the same time, we already see a growing inequality between the income of employees and those who live from profits.

Conclusion

This chapter has explored the following question: 'How does the workplace of the future constitute an aspect of the Fourth Industrial Revolution?' The short answer is that we are witnessing the development of four types of workers: the precariat, the working poor, innovation workers and knowledge workers. We have structured these four types of workers into a typology. We have described, analysed and discussed each of the four types.

What we can say at a more general level is that robotization will transform all the familiar aspects of our working lives. In only a few years from now, robots will have taken over most of the functions that we currently take for granted as part of our jobs. There will be changes in all sectors. Farming will be digitized and robotized. Already we see farmers using drones to make aspects of their work easier and safer. Tractors will be increasingly self-driven. Drones will monitor how fast crops are growing, identify pests and conduct precision-spraying in order to combat plant diseases.

Many of the same developments will apply to fisheries. Instead of flying drones, we may envisage submarine drones that detect shoals of fish and tell robots on deck how, when and at what depth to cast the nets. The boats will not even need to be crewed in order to return to shore. A completely automated fishing boat is just as realistic a prospect as a self-driven bus. In industry, industrial robots have greatly changed the nature of many jobs. In the service industry, Manchester Airport now has a robot cleaner. We already have robots that care for elderly and sick people.

Hospitals will change character. There will be no need for large hospitals to establish a greater competence environment. Compact 'hospital trailers' will be able to carry out diagnosis, medication and surgical procedures, as well as follow up and perform corrective procedures if required.

In the education industry, this will be completely globalized, especially from around 2025 when we will see the emergence of simultaneous interpretation robots that use nano-technology and are implanted in the ear without being visible. When, not if, this happens, we will experience global competition at university level. In such a scenario, we will truly experience university educational programmes at various levels.

Robots will take care of the growing elderly population, and robots will make life qualitatively better for disabled people. One might ask what type of education young people should embark on today to prepare them for the Fourth Industrial Revolution. The only answer that can be given is that you should take a long education, preferably at a university ranked high on a global scale, and a postgraduate degree such as Master's or a PhD. What field of study you choose is of less importance; the basic rule is that you should do what you are passionate about and good at. If, on the other hand, you want to start your own business in the global economy, you should take a year or two to travel around the world to investigate what's lacking and which problems you want to solve, because all innovation is based on a problem or lack of something.

Whatever you choose to do in the future, new technology will be an essential part of what you will be dealing with. On the other hand, technology is not the most important factor for the young person deciding what to do with their future. It is to learn how to think, which will distinguish the person who is successful from the one who isn't. The reasons are straightforward. In a world where everything is digitized and education is linked to robots, informats and artificial intelligence, the person with a unique competence will be able to think differently, and at the same time understand how others think. It is this competence that will create that which is innovative, and succeed, with both innovations and new businesses. It is these people who will manage 'merging concepts', which are crucial to creating the new that the world has not seen before.

With regard to future education, it is probable that a type of hybrid education linked to classical subjects such as philosophy, creativity and philology will emerge, and capture a large share of the market. Examples of possible hybrids are philosophy, technology and culture, or biology, technology and philosophy. The hybrids will make it possible to merge and create a new synthesis of concepts. This is important because innovations almost always occur at the boundaries between the various disciplines, for instance bio-technology, nano-technology, etc.

A positive development at the start of the Fourth Industrial Revolution is that technology and international trade have resulted in, among other things, 400 million of China's population emerging from poverty, and about 200 million well-off people in the growing middle class in that country, with a similar income to the middle class in the industrialized countries. In addition, the percentage of people in the world living in extreme poverty and suffering from hunger has been greatly reduced.

Despite of these developments in countries such as China, we have witnessed an ever-increasing transformation of the work of millions of people around the world, because of digitization, robotization, informatization and global free-trade capitalism forcing people out of work.

Robotization will most likely crush the middle class in the west, and move them to other parts of the social hierarchy, such as the precariat, the working poor, as recipients of a citizen salary, and in a few cases they will advance to the salaried elite.

There are four scenarios that will probably develop in the Fourth Industrial Revolution. First, there is much to suggest that there will be a development towards some form of citizen salary being paid to a country's inhabitants. Second, one can also imagine a reorganising of the workday from, for example, eight hours to four hours. The third scenario is that we will witness mass unemployment. The fourth scenario is linked to the first three. The fourth scenario is based on the four working groups we have described, analysed and discussed in this chapter.

The fourth scenario sees the development of a whole new structure of working life. A small propertied class, about 1 per cent of the population, will be super-rich. A small percentage will belong to the salaried élite. Then we envisage a large precariat that live from selling their expertise and labour through temporary contracts. At the bottom we have the working poor who will need several temporary part-time jobs just to survive. Outside of this hierarchy, we will have those living on a small citizen's salary. We have illustrated this new social stratification in Figure 1.5.

The trend we are witnessing gives rise to the following question: 'Will we see the development of technologically driven unemployment due to robots, informats and artificial intelligence?' There can be no doubt that it is unskilled workers who are under threat from the technological developments, the first outlines of which we are now seeing. The next important question to investigate is: 'How can we ensure a decent standard of living for those who, for various reasons, drop out of education?'

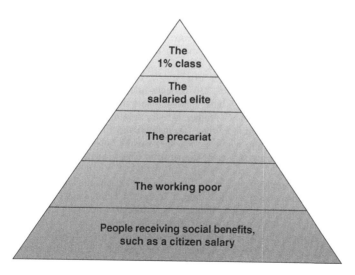

Figure 1.5 The new social stratification in the Fourth Industrial Revolution.

Notes

1 The Danish newspaper, *Politikken* (26 February 2017) refers to a report finding that the jobs most likely to proliferate are those with an average monthly pay of DNK 70,000 and those with an average monthly pay of DNK 20,000.

2 The word 'robot' was created in 1920 by the Czech author Karel Capek in his play *Rossum's Universal Robots*. The word is an amalgamation of two words: the Old Church Slavonic word *rabota*, which means servitude, and *robotnik*, which is a Czech word for slave. In Capek's play, robots are a new class of artificial people who are enslaved by humans.

3 Informats are robots that are globally interconnected.

4 www.oxfordmartin.ox.ac.uk/downloads/commission/Oxford_Martin_Now_for_the_Long_Term.pdf.

5 Ross was part of both the Clinton and the Obama administrations.

6 The term 'precariat' is derived from precarious, meaning insecure/risky. In an employment context, it is difficult for holders of precarious jobs to plan for the future.

7 Guy Standing, interview with *Politikken*, 28 August 2016.

8 'I protect, therefore I obligate.'

9 Guy Standing, interview with *Politikken*, 28 August 2016.

10 Guy Standing, interview with *Politikken*, 28 August 2016.

11 *The Independent*, 14 November, 2015.

12 See the report 'Freelancing in America' referred to in Meister and Mulcahy (2017: xiv).

13 Many of these websites are mentioned in Meister and Mulcahy (2017).

14 Quoted in Ainley (2014: 26).

15 Renana Jhabvala in 'The self-employed women's association of India' in the reviews, in the first pages of Standing (2014a).

16 https://en.wikipedia.org/wiki/Mini_job (date of access: 3 March 2017).

17 https://en.wikipedia.org/wiki/Mini_job (date of access: 3 March2017).

18 The description of the Hartz reforms was accessed from: https://en.wikipedia.org/wiki/Hartz_concept (date of access: 2 January 2017).

19 https://en.wikipedia.org/wiki/Hartz_concept (date of access: 3 March 2017).

20 The strategy was developed around 1988 when Deng Xioping formulated the thesis that China should export to increase the country's wealth by allowing foreign investors to invest in China. His idea was: it doesn't matter what colour the cat is as long as it can catch mice. The explanation is that capitalists can invest in China as long as the Communist Party is in control of social development and they can make China into a rich country (Pantsov, 2017).

21 By the end of 2004, there were 2236 colleges and universities, with over 20 million students enrolled in mainland China.[1] More than 6 million Chinese students graduated from university in 2008.[2] The 'Project 211' for creating 100 universities began in the mid-1990s, and has merged more than 700 institutions of higher learning into about 300 universities. Corresponding with the merging of many public universities, has been the rapid expansion of the private sector in mainland China since 1999. As of 2006, private universities accounted for around 6 per cent of student enrolments, or about 1.3 million of the 20 million students enrolled in formal higher education (https://en.wikipedia.org/wiki/List_of_universities_in_China, date of access: 21 February 2017).

22 There are numerous indications that robots, informats and artificial intelligence will take over most of the work activities that people now perform. Among those who have written about this development are Standing (2014: viii); Meister and Mulcahy (2017: 189); Coates and Morrison (2016: 23–59); Grain et al. (2016); Ross (2016: 19–32); Bond (2013).

23 The figures are from Ross (2016: 41).

24 *Politikken* at the end of February 2016.

25 *Politikken*, 24 February 2017.
26 *Politikken*, 24 February 2017.
27 *Politikken*, 24 February 2017.
28 Moore's law states that computing power will double every second year.

References

Abd, K.K. (2017). Intelligent scheduling of robotic flexible assembly cells, Springer, London.

Abrahamson, M. (2004). Global cities, Oxford University Press, Oxford.

Ackoff, R.L. (1989). Re-creating the corporate future, Oxford University Press, Oxford.

Ainley, P. (2014). Follow your dreams and attend to universities if possible, Latitude, 21 December.

Ainley, P. (2016). Betraying a generation: How education is failing young people, Policy Press, Bristol.

Allen, M. (2004). The rise and fall of the GNVQ: Young people and vocational qualifications at the start of the twenty-first century, PhD thesis, Open University, Milton Keynes.

Armano, E. & Murgia, A. (2015). The precariousness of young knowledge workers: A subject-oriented approach, in Johnson, M. (ed.). Precariat: Labour, work and politics, Routledge, London, pp.102–117.

Arnold, D. (2005). Exploiting in global supply chains: Burmese migrant workers in Mae Sot, Thailand, Journal of Contemporary Asia, 35, 3: 319–340.

Arnold, D. (2013). Social margins and precarious work in Vietnam, American Behavioral Scientist, 57, 4: 468–487.

Arnold, D. & Bongiovi, J.R. (2013). Precarious, informalizing, and flexible work: transforming concepts and understandings, American Behavioral Scientist, 57, 3: 289–308.

Atkinson, W. (2010). The myth of the reflexive worker: Class and work histories in neoliberal times, Work, Employment & Society, 24, 3: 413–429.

Avent, R. (2016). The wealth of humans: Work and its absence in the twenty-first century, Allen Lane, New York.

Banki, S. (2015). Precarity of place: A complement to the growing precariat literature, in Johnson, M. (ed.). Precariat: Labour, work and politics, Routledge, London, pp.66–79.

Bennis, W.G., Cloke, K. & Goldsmith, J. (2012). The end of management and the rise of organisational democracy, John Wiley & Sons, New York.

Bleuer, H., Bouri, M. & Mandada, F.C. (2017). New trends in medical and service robots, Springer, London.

Bolanski, L. & Chiapello, E. (2017). The new spirit of capitalism, Verso, London.

Bond, J. (2013). Robot report predicts significant growth in coming decade, Logistic Management, April 25.

Boxall, P.F. & Purcell, J. (2010). An HRM perspective on employee participation, in Wilkinson, A., Golan, P.J., Marchington, M. & Lewins, D. (eds). The Oxford handbook of participation in organisations, Oxford University Press, Oxford, pp.129–151.

Bratianu, C. (2015). Organisational knowledge dynamics, Information Science Reference, New York.

Bruce, D. & Crook, G. (2015). The dream café: Lessons in the art of radical Innovation, John Wiley & Sons, New York.

Brynjolfsson, E. & McAfee, A. (2011). Race against the machine, Digital Frontier Press, New York.

Brynjolfsson, E. & McAfee, A. (2014). The second machine age, W.W. Norton & Company, New York.

Case, S. (2016). The third wave, Simon & Schuster, New York.

Chomsky, N. (2012). How the world works, Hamish Hamilton, London.

Chomsky, N. (2016a). Who rules the world, Hamish Hamilton, London.

Chomsky, N. (2016b). Profit over people: War against people, Piper, Berlin.

Christensen, C.M. (2016). The Clayton M. Christensen reader, Harvard Business School Press, Boston.

Coates, K.S. & Morrison, B. (2016). Dream factories, TAP Books, Toronto.

De Sario, B. (2007). Precari Su Marte: An experiment in activism against precarity, Feminist Review, 87, 1: 21–39.

Dorling, D. (2015). Inequality and the 1%, Verso, London.

Drucker, P.F. (1999a). Knowledge worker productivity: The biggest challenge, California Management Review, 41, 2: 79–94.

Drucker, P.F. (1999b). Management challenges for the 21st century, Harper Collins, New York.

Du Gay, P. & Morgan, G. (ed.). (2004). New spirits of capitalism? Crises, justification and dynamics, Oxford University Press, Oxford.

Florida, R. (2002). The rise of the creative class and how its transforming work, life, community and everyday life, Basic Books, New York.

Frey, C.B. & Osborne, M.A. (2013). The future of employment: How susceptible are jobs to computerization, Oxford Martin School Press, Oxford.

Gans, J. (2016). The disruption dilemma, MIT Press, Boston, MA.

Gant, A. (2014). Give and take, why helping others drives our success, W&N, New York.

Garud, R., Kumaraswamy, A. & Langlois, R. (2002). Managing in the modular age: New perspectives on architectures, networks and organisations, Wiley-Blackwell, New York.

Gaskarth, J. (Red.). (2015). China, India and the future of international society, Rowman & Littlefield, London.

Goldberg, K. (2000). The robot in the garden: Telerobotics and telepistemology in the age of the internet, MIT Press, Boston, MA.

Grain, M.G., Poster, W.R. & Cherry, M.A. (eds.). (2016). Invisible labor, University of California Press, Oakland, CA.

Grant, A.M. (2014). Give and take, W&N, New York.

Gratton, L. (2011). The shift, Collins, London.

Hochschild, A. (2016). Forward: Invisible labor, inaudible voice, in Grain, M.G., Poster, W.R. & Cherry, M.A. (eds). Invisible labor, University of California Press, Oakland, CA, pp.xi–xiv.

Howe, J. (2006). Crowdsourcing, Wired, June.

Ikonen, K.-M. (2015). Precarious work, entrepreneurial mindset and the sense of place: Female strategies in insecure labour markets, in Johnson, M. Precariat: Labour, work and politics, Routledge, London, pp.83–97.

Johannessen, J.-A. (1979). Industrialisering av torskefiskeriene i Nord-Troms og Finnmark, Universitetet i Oslo, Kandidatavhandling, Oslo.

Johnson, M. (2015b). Introduction, the precariat, in Johnson, M. (ed.). Precariat: Labour, work and politics, Routledge, London, pp.1–3.

Kessler, S. (2017). Gigged: The end of jobs and the future of work, Random House Business, New York.

Lane, C.M. (2011). A company of one: Insecurity, independence and the new world of white-collar unemployment, ILR Press, New York.

Lazzarato, M. (2012). The making of indebted man: An essay of the neoliberal condition, Semiotexte, San Francisco, CA.

Lessard, M. & Baldwin, S. (2000). Net slaves: True tales of working the web, McGraw-Hill, New York.

Mason, P. (2012). Why it's kicking off everywhere: The new global revolutions, Verso, New York.

McAffee, A. & Brynjolfsson, E. (2017). Machine platform: Harnessing the digital revolution, W.W. Norton & Company, New York.

McGill, K. (2016). Global inequality, University of Toronto Press, Toronto.

Meister, J.C. & Mulcahy, K.J. (2017). The future workplace experience, McGraw Hill, New York.

Monbiot, G. (2016). How did we get into this mess? Politics, equality, nature, Verso, London.

Morris, J. (2012). Unruly entrepreneurs: Russian worker responses to insecure formal employment, Global Labour Journal, 3, 2: 217–236.

Murphy, A. (2016). The optimistic workplace, Amacom, New York.

Otis, E.O. & Zhao, Z. (2016). Production, invisibility: Surveillance, hunger and work in the produce aisles of Wal-Mart, China, in Grain, M.G.; Poster, W.R. & Cherry, M.A. (eds). Invisible labor, University of California Press, Oakland, CA, pp.148–169.

Pantsov, A. (2017). Deng Xiaoping: A revolutionary life, Oxford University Press, New York.

Perlin, R. (2011). Intern nation: How to earn nothing and learn little in the brave new economy, Verso, London.

Pongratz, H.J. & Voss, G. (2003). From employee to entreployee: Towards a self-entrepreneurial work force, Concepts and Transformation, 8, 3: 239–254.

Poster, W.R. (2016). The virtual receptionist with a human touch, in Grain, M.G., Poster, W. R. & Cherry, M.A. (eds). Invisible labor, University of California Press, Oakland, CA, pp.87–113.

Reich, R. (2015). Saving capitalism, Icon, New York.

Reinmoell, S. & Reinmoeller, P. (2015). The ambidextrous organisation, Routledge, Oxford.

Ross, A. (2009). Nice work if you can get it: Life and labor in precarious times, New York University Press, New York.

Ross, A. (2016). The industries of the future, Simon & Schuster, New York.

Rothkopf, D. (2009). Superclass: The global power elite and the world they are making, Strauss and Giroux, New York.

Rothkopf, D. (2012). Power, Inc: The epic rivalry between big business and government- and the reckoning that lies ahead, Straus and Giroux, New York.

Samek Lodovici, M. & Semenza, R. (2012). Precarious work and high-skilled youth in Europe, Angeli, Milano.

Savage, M. (2015). Social class in the 21st century, Penguin, London.

Sennett, R. (2006). The culture of the new capitalism, Yale University Press, New Heaven, London.

Shipler, D. (2005). The working poor, Vintage, New York.

Standing, G. (2014a). The precariat: The new dangerous class, Bloomsbury Academic, New York.

Standing, G. (2014b). A precariat charter, Bloomsbury, London.

Steiner, C. (2012). Automate this, Penguin, New York.

Stewart, E. (2016). Simply white: Race, politics, and invisibility in advertising depictions of farm labor, in Grain, M.G., Poster, W.R. & Cherry, M.A. (eds). Invisible labor, University of California Press, Oakland, CA, pp.120–148.

Surowiecki, J. (2005). The wisdom of crowds: Why the many are smarter than the few, Abacus, New York.

Susskind, R. & Susskind, D. (2015). The future of professions: How technology will transform the work of human experts, Oxford University Press, Oxford.

Swider, S. (2015). Building China, Informal work and the new, ILR Press, London.

Tapia, A. (2009). The inclusion paradox: The Obama era and the transformation of global diversity, Hewit Associates, Lincolnshire.

Tarrow, S. (2005). The new transnational activism, Cambridge University Press, Cambridge.

Tolonen, T. (2005). Locality and gendered capital of working-class youth, Young, 13, 4: 343–361.

Trot, B. (2015). From the precariat to the multitude, in Johnson, M. (ed.). Precariat: Labour, work and politics, Routledge, London, pp.22–41.

Turkle, S. (2016). Reclaiming the conversation, The power of talk in the digital age, Penguin, New York.

Varga, J.J. (2015). Breaking the heartland creating the precariat in the US lower rust belt, in Johnson, M. (ed.). Precariat: Labour, work and politics, Routledge, London, pp.46–62.

Wacquant, L. (2009a). Punishing the poor, Duke University Press, London.

Wacquant, L. (2009b). Prisons of poverty, University of Minnesota Press, New York.

Wakeling, P. & Savage, M. (2015). Entry to elite positions and the stratification of higher education in Britain, Sociological Review, 63, 2: 290–320.

Wakeling, P. & Savage, M. (2015a). Elite universities, elite schooling and reputation in Britain, in Zanten, A.V. & Ball, S. (eds). Elites, privilege and excellence: The national and global redefinition of educational advantage, World Yearbook of Education, Abingdon, London.

Wang, R. (2015). Disrupting digital business: Create an authentic experience in the peer-to peer economy, Harvard Business Review Press, Boston, MA.

Wilson, M. (2017). Implementation of robot systems, Butterworth-Heinemann, New York.

Xie, S. (2017). Advanced robotics for medical rehabilitation, Springer, London.

Zhao, J., Feng, Z., Chu, F. & Ma, N. (2017). Advanced theory of constraint and motion analysis for robot mechanisms, Academic Press, London.

2 New organizational logic and the future of work

Introduction

In order to understand the Fourth Industrial Revolution (Schwab, 2016), we must be able to describe and explain the emergence of the knowledge society. Robots and informats[1] cause changes in employment structures: old jobs are destroyed and new ones created; work is disrupted and transformed. These trends are a direct outcome of the transition to the Fourth Industrial Revolution (Arrow, 2012; Abd, 2017; Xie, 2017). New jobs are being created with completely new kinds of content (Zhao et al., 2017), and new businesses are starting up at an unknown rate (Hamel, 2012; Christensen, 2016). The decline of industrial employment in the west, and the increasing opportunities for employment in information-related jobs and the service sector are an outcome of the informatization and automation of work (Acemoglu, 2003; Barrat, 2015; Ross, 2016). The increasing information- and knowledge-related content of jobs is an expression of the emergence of a new organizational logic, with its own specific characteristics: lego flexibility and experience design (Baird & Henderson, 2001; Meister & Mulcahy, 2017). Lego flexibility means, among other things, that the production chain will be outsourced to several countries in accordance with a cost, quality, innovation and competence logistic (Susskind & Susskind, 2015; Wiedemer et al., 2015). By the same logic, the administrative system, and therefore the various roles of staff members, can also be thought of as being outsourced.

Experience design is an innovative management and organizational model, on which the focus is on processes and the coupling of customers and workers who do what the organization is designed to do, i.e. the people on the frontline (Hamel, 2008; Armstrong, 2014a). This model seems to be gaining ground, at the expense of bureaucratic and hierarchical principles (Sassen, 2015). Various forms of experience-based design seem to be establishing themselves as the dominant pattern (Srinivasa, 2017).

The main question in this chapter is: 'How can new organizational logic create wealth in the emergence of the Fourth Industrial Revolution?'

We have divided this question into two sub-questions:

1. How can new lego flexibility create wealth in the emergence of the Fourth Industrial Revolution?

2. How can experience design create wealth in the emergence of the Fourth Industrial Revolution?

This is illustrated in Figure 2.1, which also shows how the rest of the chapter is organized.

Lego flexibility

First we describe and then analyse and discuss lego flexibility, creating a sub-conclusion.

Descriptions

Lego flexibility means that the production of every product is broken down into its component parts. These components are produced where the cost is low, the quality high, the competence excellent, and the innovation rate above average and high (Garud et al., 2002; Sennett, 2006, 2009). Each of these four elements brings different components from different parts of the world, but they are finally brought together to make up the product, which could be a mobile phone, a car, a computer, etc.

Lego flexibility depends on the existence of an organizational form in which multifunctional teams form the smallest units and global competence clusters form the global unit (Azmat, 2012). In addition, it is vital to assign a central role to knowledge development, knowledge transfer, feedback processes, co-creation and the analysis of social sentiment (Susskind & Susskind, 2015; Meister & Mulcahy, 2017).

Information, communication and technology functions could be outsourced, for example, to the Bangalore region in India, sales functions to Paris, London and New York, PR and media relations to Berkeley and administrative functions to Berlin. One could also envisage such a strong focus on core processes that all other functions are spinoffs brought in for strictly limited activities for a specific assignment.

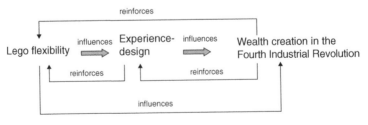

Figure 2.1 Wealth creation processes in the Fourth Industrial Revolution.

There will be enormous social consequences if this type of lego flexibility does come into effect globally (Standing, 2014a, 2014b), and it will represent the development of a new form of global work distribution and professional specialization (Gaskarth, 2015). In this new landscape, competence development, career development, personal risk and wealth-creation processes will all undergo inherent change. One result of this kind of lego flexibility will be that sovereign states could easily lose their grip over wealth-creation processes (Stearns, 2013; Kessler, 2017). As we know from the industrial era, democratic control over wealth-creation processes can easily disintegrate, erode and be downgraded to a purely symbolic level (Gutmann & Thompson, 1996; Gershuny & Fisher, 2014a).

In the 1980s and 1990s a large part of the workforce moved from industrial production to jobs in the service and knowledge sectors (Enderwick, 1989; Foster, 2014). This movement occurred both through cuts in the number of traditional production jobs and an increase in service and knowledge jobs (Thurow, 1999: 216). On the threshold of the Fourth Industrial Revolution, knowledge workers – making up the backbone of the middle class – are now under threat (Coates & Morrison, 2016), as are service workers (Frey & Osborne, 2013).

We analyse and discuss how this development in the new organizational logic result in new forms of cooperation, the main driver of which is the new technology, i.e. robots, informats and artificial intelligence (AI) (Stanford, 2013; Wilson, 2017).

Analysis and discussion

Lego flexibility, with its consequences such as cutbacks, outsourcing of functions, and its focus on core activities, increased job insecurity and acquisitions to achieve global competitiveness, will lead to knowledge and service workers becoming extremely vulnerable (Ford, 2016; Kessler, 2017). This feeling of vulnerability, failure and inadequacy may soon become the norm (Bernstein, 1996; Gans, 2016). Education and risk-taking will not be enough to succeed, and tightly packed small social networks will be critical to success in the Fourth Industrial Revolution (Garza, 2013). In addition, we should not ignore random components, although prepared individuals will be better placed to take advantage of any random situations that may arise than those who are not prepared through education, social networks, political networks and the willingness to take risks (Gratton, 2011: 105–133).

A consequence of lego flexibility is a feeling of inadequacy, failure, and that one's career is not moving in the right direction, and one is a victim of unforeseeable forces. The reason for this is that lego flexibility increases complexity and turbulence in the global economy to a great degree (Goodman, 2015), and also that education will no longer be a sufficient criterion for success, as was the case in the industrial economy (Gupta et al., 2016).

The system of relationships one enters into, i.e. social networks, will become increasingly important for success (Gershuny & Fisher, 2014). The importance of building relationships applies at both the individual and the corporate level (Foster, 2014), as relationships will enable co-creation, both between individuals and between customers and the company (Fairtlough, 2007).

Lego flexibility also means that power will be concentrated, but wealth-creation processes will be distributed (Goodman, 2015). Social ties between the various modules will be weak, and could easily lead to consequences for collective solutions, because individualization will be promoted by this lack of social ties (Chomsky, 2016a, 2016b). Neither individuals nor the nation state will have the 'requisite variety' (Ashby, 1961) needed to cope with the power of finance capital (Sennett, 2013a, 2013b; Piketty, 2016). One consequence of this development may be that identity will change from association with trade unions and the nation to small dense social networks built on collaborative deployment over time (Gutmann & Thompson, 1996; Gollan, 2010).

Another way of analysing the development of lego flexibility is through responsibility and the social dimension. Responsibility for others will be characterized by relationships within dense, small, robust, social networks (Sennett, 2013a, 2013b), which will maintain the social and material security while providing identity in the new lego flexibility. These networks will also cover the psychological need for belonging and feeling needed (Brynjolfsson & McAfee, 2014).

Lego flexibility may lead to weak ties. If structural connections between social systems are weak, then a crisis in one place in the global economy will not necessarily be transferred to another place of equal strength and depth, as is the case when structural connections are strong (Case, 2016). On the contrary, it could be the case that, if structural connections are weak, then some areas may profit from a crisis elsewhere. A crisis can also trigger cost advantages in the crisis-hit areas, which after some time may gain competitive advantages (Evans & Schmalensee, 2016). In this way, economic crises may be viewed as a cleansing process that strengthens the social system once the crisis has subsided.

Lego flexibility is enhanced by new technology, i.e. robots, informats and AI. This development will demand new competences and new forms of cooperation, which will drive wealth-creation processes, and ensure greater prosperity for some who participate in the new workplace pyramid (Fairtlough, 2007; McAffee & Brynjolfsson, 2017). At the top of this pyramid are the wage nobility (Kessler, 2017), followed by the precariat (Standing, 2014a, 2014b; Johnson, 2015), and with 'The working poor' at the bottom (Shipler, 2005). Outside the workplace pyramid we find the 1 per cent who own most of the value creation processes (Dorling, 2015; Wilkins, 2016)

We have seen a larger than usual differential in salary trends and incomes (Dorling, 2015; Wilkin, 2016; Piketty, 2016), while at the same time productivity in the service sector has been very low (Susskind & Susskind, 2015). Lego flexibility will not decrease these trends. Another important point is that the concept of productivity is in itself in doubt when we talk about the knowledge economy and lego flexibility, because turbulence and new organizational structures promote the development of other concepts such as indicators to measure performance, e.g. innovation, flexibility, adaptability, relational and networking competence, and the tackling of complexity and ambiguity (Fisher, 2006; Gershuny & Fisher, 2014).

If a social system cannot manage the pace of restructuring, i.e. to lego flexibility, then it is highly likely that this will result in social consequences at the individual level (Standing, 2014a; Bleuer et al., 2017)., i.e. one should be aware of the trends and act accordingly (Brynjolfsson & McAfee, 2014). Struggling against this logic may well give your life meaning, but such a struggle may be likened to Sisyphus eternally rolling his boulder up a hill, only to watch it roll back down again destroying everything in its path. A more productive approach is to be innovative within the framework of new creative network constellations and adapt to trends that are created by others (Case, 2016). One could say: 'Create your own future or others will create it for you' (Ackoff, 1989).

Economic logic in the globalized era has had the whole globe as a friction-free market, and this lego flexibility is just one of the consequences of this development. In this new reality, wealth-creation processes have changed character from a logic of production to a logic of global competence clusters (Srinivasa, 2017).

Sub-conclusion

The research question was: How can new lego flexibility create wealth in the emergence of the Fourth Industrial Revolution?

The above description, discussion and analysis have been summarized in Figure 2.2,and provides the answer to our research question.

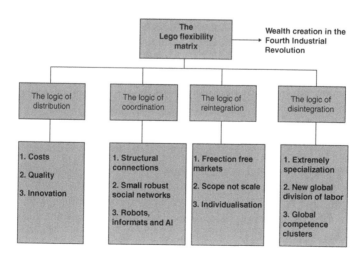

Figure 2.2 The lego flexibility matrix.

Experience-design and wealth creation

First we describe, and then analyse and discuss experience-design and wealth creation, creating a sub-conclusion.

Descriptions

A key aim of the new organizational logic developing in the Fourth Industrial Revolution, regardless of from where the driving forces are coming, is to take responsibility, and develop creativity in the surrounding environment and the global competence network, in order to create innovations (Brynjolfsson & McAfee, 2014). The new organization will look like something that is non-hierarchical, non-bureaucratic but focused on experience at the frontline, and exists between customers and people on the frontline. This organizing principle is called experience-design (Meister & Mulcahy, 2017: xiii–xxx). Experience-design demands, however, the development of mutual respect in the social system, where human values are fundamental to the wealth-creation processes. This is because in a network it is easy for the weakest link to become the one that causes the whole network to reduce its capacity; as a result every participant must base their behaviour on certain fundamental values in which individuals experience well-being from their position within the network and the wealth-creation processes. This must in no way be confused with equality, or an egalitarian system, or any particular brand of politics (Bauman, 2013). The question we address through this line of argument is: 'What possibilities does the individual possess to realize a given set of generally accepted values?' (The values referred to are, for instance, respect, responsibility and dignity (Benhabib, 2002, 2004; Benhabib et al., 2006).)

If the individual feels that the values in the experience-design are in agreement with their values, then it will function according to its purpose. If, however, the individual feels the opposite, then the structure of the experience-design must be changed, in order to increase the likelihood of a positive answer to the question.

When people at the frontline can make decisions in real time, this needs a strong focus on two aspects: first, competence and maintenance of competence at the frontline, which applies to individual competence, team competence and not least organization of the business so that the frontline always has support, serviced and assistance at all levels. Second, it needs coordination between activities to be optimized at the system and network levels. The new organizational logic constitutes a transition from functions via cross-functional teams to process organization, where the customer, user and citizen (the public) are placed at the centre, and this centre is organized around the frontline. This design is called here experience-design, because the experience between the customer and the frontline people happens here. Figure 2.3 shows schematically what we have described.

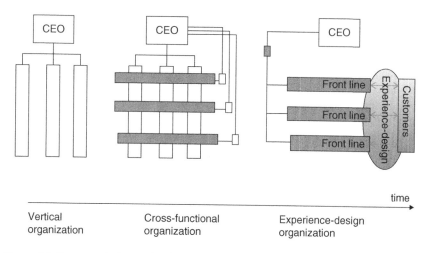

time

| Vertical | Cross-functional | Experience-design |
| organization | organization | organization |

Figure 2.3 From vertical organization in hierarchies to process organization towards the frontline.

Analysis and discussion

In many organizations the frontline is being upgraded in order to interact with other players in the global sphere (Stanford, 2013; Susskind & Susskind, 2015). Experiences with customers is always at the frontline (Ramaswamy & Ozcan, 2014; Robertson, 2015). In the industrial society the bureaucratic system was important as a stabilizing and coordinating factor, but, in the knowledge society, frontline competence is the crucial factor for wealth creation and connection with creative and innovative networks (Bleuer et al., 2017). Accordingly, it is at the frontline that 'sense and response' mechanisms must be developed to capture, and make use of, the stream of experiences that will ensure survival of the system (Brynjolfsson & McAfee, 2011; Bleuer et al., 2017). If it is true that information, experience-design and frontline focus are essential for wealth creation in the Fourth Industrial Revolution, then competence at the frontline will become essential for survival (Mason, 2015). A necessary condition for this is the downscaling of bureaucratic structures, which should occur rapidly and forcefully, because of robots, informats and AI (Noonan & Nadkarny, 2016; Wilson, 2017). If this doesn't occur, then bureaucracy will slow down the necessary restructuring processes, and be a cost-increasing element (Pink, 2001). Creativity and innovation are essential for wealth creation in the knowledge economy (Brynjolfsson & Saunders, 2013). Bureaucracy, with its constraining and stabilizing thought mode, cannot follow the new transformations that take place, because the speed, flexibility and decision-making skills in real time are not part of the rational bureaucratic model (Bunge, 2015: 261).

Frontline focus, free agents, e-lance (not freelance but e-work), small, tightly packed social networks, intrapreneurship, entrepreneurship, innovative entrepreneurship, etc. can deal much better with the new challenges and opportunities than traditional bureaucratic organizations (Susskind & Susskind, 2015; Meister & Mulcahy, 2017). The Fourth Industrial Revolution will be network connected, multi-faceted, and adapted to various emerging opportunities and the equally rapid disappearance of the same opportunities (Schwab, 2016). One common feature of the Fourth Industrial Revolution could gel as structural connections that rapidly change character in relation to emerging needs in real time (Ross, 2016). This will need competence as a primary factor to cope with complexities result from the flexibility of the structural connections (Armstrong, 2014a, 2014b). When competence at the frontline becomes the primary factor, and the frontline becomes synonymous with decisions made in the social system, then bureaucracy will inevitably become superfluous. Competence at the frontline, and collective learning structures among businesses, customers and suppliers, in addition to flexibility in operating networks and new technology, will form the basis of the knowledge economy's wealth-creation processes (Autor et al., 2003).

Robot technology, informats and systemically linked nano-computers will enable individualized and customized solutions, so that niche production will become a reality for manufacturers as a result of the global market (Abd, 2017; Bleuer et al., 2017; Wilson, 2017). Although the customer base and variety in what they demand will increase sharply, new technology will enable a complete, individualized relationship with each customer/user (Lima, 2017). The individual's profile will form the basis for a business's referrals to the customer, and the customer will generate their profile through contact with the business. This experience-design will then co-create wealth for both the customers and the organizations.

It is technology that will create and modify the customer's profile, so customer satisfaction will constantly be maximized (Ross, 2016). Individual relationships and customized solutions for customers will function as a strong competitive advantage in a development where social ties elsewhere in society become weaker (Sennett, 2006, 2009, 2013a, 2013b). Examples of products/services that can be individualized are in the medical field, computers and computer software, the garment industry, safety equipment, groceries, music, books, entertainment, news, education, elderly care, etc. (Ford, 2016; Abd, 2017: Xie, 2017).

Individualization may also lead to customers reducing expenditure, because they will get exactly what they need and no more. This could increase customer satisfaction and re-purchases may be developed (Winfield, 2012). To achieve this requires, among other things, deliverability skills. To produce what the customers want, while still being able to deliver on time, will be an important criterion for success (Robertson, 2015). A frontline focus and customized solutions will thus become two important factors for achieving this. Adaptation to the individual customer requires an innovative system that is focused on continuous change and co-creation among the system, customer and supplier (Brynjolfsson & McAfee, 2014).

Those businesses that manage to build an organization and working methods connected to the new technology, to customize their products/ services, will be in front of the Fourth Industrial Revolution. To this end, organizing is just as important as technology (Brynjolfsson & McAfee, 2014; Case, 2016).

The new technology (robots, AI and informats) increasingly enables individualized service. Customers can now more easily be classified by contact, and directed to the specific staff to handle the individualized solutions to the customer's request. Customers no longer have to be exposed to the internal processes and they can be directed to the specific staff at the frontline with the expertise to deal with their request. In the future their requests will be answered by robots in real time without delay (Abd, 2017; Bleuer et al., 2017; Wilson, 2017). Viewed from this perspective, technology will be used to differentiate customers so that the service is appropriate to the individual customer (Barrat, 2015; Xie, 2017). In this way, the products/ services will literally be customized for each customer. Re-purchase by the existing customer base will also become a criterion for success when the customer is the critical factor (Ramaswamy & Ozcan, 2014). Consequently, every transaction with the customer will lead to experience transfer and learning by the system, so at the next point of transaction the customer will have a new updated profile. Such a experience-design in which a customer-learning system can be employed in several areas, such as the sale of books, music, films, news, entertainment, clothing, research services, educational services, groceries, furniture, library services, banking, medical services, lawyers services, teachers services etc., will increase business results (Robertson, 2015; Wilson, 2017).

It is rather a question of which areas cannot be covered by the new customizing robotic systems. An important point with such customer-learning systems is to retain the customer by either providing products and services or offering what customers are looking for in the network that the business is a part. The business must therefore offer links to other businesses, which must be included in a network where such a return of favours is part of its function. This can be done by digital machines, robots, informats using AI and other organizational techniques.

The relationship with the customer is a direct one, and the business adapts its products and services to the individual customer. This relationship can be more efficient with robots and informats than with personal contact. By offering other links to the customer, learning will increase further, because the business would gain a larger and better overall profile of each customer than would be possible if the profile were created only around the products/services supplied by the business (Stanford, 2013). Being a total information provider is therefore very important for the individual business, with the aim always to provide services in relation to all the customer's needs, and thus psychologically binding the customer to the business. This binding is done by linking the customer via robots and informats with the global system, through the hotspot of the single company. The customer must experience information offered by the business as relevant; if not, information delivery will be perceived as negative (Hislop, 2013).

One consequence of the individualized customization and upgrading of competence in the frontline is, among other things, a transition from hierarchical management and control systems to more vertical systems of organization and management (Hlupic, 2014).

The key features of the new organizational logic resulting from the frontline focus and customization may be as follows:

* Process organization;
* De-bureaucratization;
* Team organization;
* A large degree of external structural links;
* Continuous competence development at all levels.

The critical factor in experience-design concerns our mental models, and how we think about the changes that have been made and the ones we know will occur in the future (Meister & Mulcahy, 2017). From such an understanding, robots, informats and AI should be considered as a means of changing the organizational logic. Performance improvements, for example in the knowledge workers' productivity, will be a result of the new organizational logic, rather than the new technology (Stanford, 2013; Susskind & Susskind, 2015; Wilson, 2017). Viewed from this perspective, the new technology will be a midwife to the new organizational logic (Kiggins, 2017). The new robot technology and the systemically linked informats, and even the nano-computers, will be the unifying glue in the organizational spider's web, which holds everything together in a very strong, systemically linked system (Johannessen, 2016b).

Sub-conclusion

The research question was: 'How can experience-design create wealth in the emergence of the Fourth Industrial Revolution?' We answered this question by focusing on the interaction between the frontline and the customers, systemically linked to robots and informats in a global competence cluster. It is this interaction that will create wealth in the Fourth Industrial Revolution.

Figure 2.4 summarizes the above description, discussion and analysis. It is also the answer to our research question.

Conclusion

The main question we investigated in this chapter is: 'How can new organizational logic create wealth in the emergence of the Fourth Industrial Revolution?'

Wealth-creation processes in the Fourth Industrial Revolution are structured around two wealth-creation elements (see Figure 2.1): lego flexibility and experience-design.

The synthesis of these elements of wealth creation and the overarching answer to our main research question are presented figuratively in Figure 2.5.

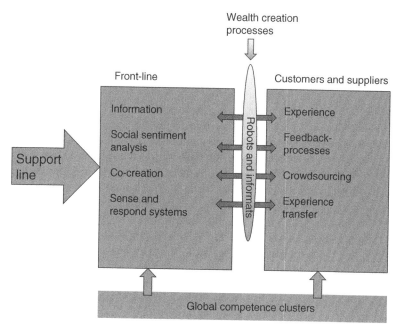

Figure 2.4 Experience-design and wealth creation.

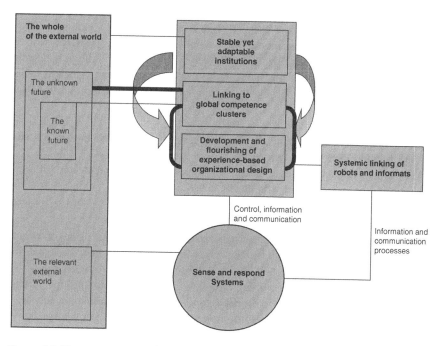

Figure 2.5 How can new organizational logic create wealth in the emergence of the Fourth Industrial Revolution?

Below, in response to the main research question, we suggest some tentative syntheses and some questions for further research.

Lego flexibility

A network logic has been the key driving force in the development of the knowledge economy. However, to a large extent it is the major multinational corporations that will play a decisive role in the development of such dynamic networks. Although one may find a number of examples where small- and medium-sized businesses have been fundamental to networking logistics, as, for example, in north Italy, there appears to be a transition from large companies towards global competence networks and global competence clusters. These global networks will focus on specialized niche companies, which act as 'Lego bricks' or modules in a global wealth-creation process. These modules are the organizational logistics that drive the development of the global competence networks, and the owners of these networks are the large-scale entities of global capitalism: funds of various types. These funds may be owned by trade unions, large pension funds, or to a small, and even insignificant, extent individuals and families. Our point is, however, that these new organizational logistics bind the fox and the hens together in the hen house in a fiendish pact: no one is served by disrupting the stability of these unstable dynamic networks.

Lego flexibility – further research

Sometimes sheep flee to escape when they see wolves coming. At other times sheep will blindly follow other sheep if they see them running. Then again, they may even flee because they mistake the wind rustling in the trees for wolves approaching. The idea here is that, if everybody or many follow the same strategy, the result may be disaster for the system as a whole, which is what happens in flocking behaviour. On this basis we ask the following questions for further research:

- In which way will global competence clusters impact the design of new information management structures?
- In which way will 'Lego bricks' or modules impact the design of new information management structures?

Experience-design

Classic industrial production will be executed by automated processes using robots and informats operated by technology workers who will work remotely from the actual site of production. The classic industrial worker will become a largely historical figure.

Information and knowledge will be interwoven into social relationships, and in many contexts will be for the collective good. Given the information networks that exist today, it is impossible to monopolize theoretical knowledge. It is produced and reproduced in a global network of information and knowledge workers, which to an ever greater extent creates value at the frontline level that it encounters, and often in collaboration with clients, customers, students, etc. This experience-design enables co-creation at the frontline, where learning will bring productivity gain and customer satisfaction.

Experience-design – future research

The global competence clusters, level of technology, infostructure and infrastructure will be decisive in success or failure in the Fourth Industrial Revolution. A danger in the knowledge economy is an absence of long-term thinking, because it is precisely long-term investments in research, infostructures, infrastructures, etc. that will be necessary in an era where thinking will be dominated by short-term interests.

On this basis we ask the following questions for further research:

- In which way will experience-design impact the design of new information management structures?
- In which way will a distinction between infostructures and infrastructures impact the design of new information management structures?

Note

1 Informats are robots that are globally interconnected.

References

Abd, K.K. (2017). Intelligent scheduling of robotic flexible assembly cells, Springer, London.

Acemoglu, D. (2003). Labor- and capital-augmenting technical change, Journal of European Economic Association, 1(1): 1–37.

Ackoff, R.L. (1989). Re-creating the corporation, Oxford University Press, Oxford.

Armstrong, M. (2014a). Armstrong's handbook of strategic human resource management, Kogan Page, New York.

Armstrong, M. (2014b). Armstrong's handbook of human resource management practice, Kogan Page, New York.

Arrow, K.J. (2012). Praise for why nations fail, in Acemoglu, D. & Robinson, J.A. (eds). Why nations fail, Grown Publisher, New York.

Ashby, W.R. (1961). An introduction to cybernetics, Chapman & Hall, New York.

Autor, D., Levy, F. & Murnane, R.J. (2003). The skill content of recent technological change: An empirical exploration, Quarterly Journal of Economics, 118, 4: 1279–1333.

Azmat, G., Manning, A. & Van Reenen, J. (2012). Privatization and the decline of the labour's share, International evidence from network industries, Economica, 79: 470–492.

Baird, L. & Henderson, J.C. (2001). The knowledge engine, Berrett-Koehler, San Francisco, CA.

Barrat, J. (2015). Our final invention, St Martin's Griffin, London.

Bauman, Z. (2013). Does the richness of the few benefit us all? Polity, London.

Benhabib, S. (2002). The claims of culture, Princeton University Press, Princeton, NJ.

Benhabib, S. (2004). The rights of others, Cambridge University Press, Cambridge.

Benhabib, S., Waldron, J., Honig, B. & Kymlicka, W. (eds) (2006). Another cosmopolitanism, Oxford University Press, Oxford.

Bernstein, P. (1996). Against the gods: The remarkable story of risk, John Wiley, New York.

Bleuer, H., Bouri, M. & Mandada, F.C. (2017). New trends in medical and service robots, Springer, London.

Brynjolfsson, E. & McAfee, A. (2011). Race against the Machine, Digital Frontier Press, New York.

Brynjolfsson, E. & McAfee, A. (2014). The second machine age, W.W Norton & Company, New York.

Brynjolfsson, E. & Saunders, A. (2013). Wired for innovation: How information technology is reshaping the economy, The MIT Press, London.

Bunge, M. (2015). Political philosophy, Transaction Publisher, New York.

Case, S. (2016). The third wave, Simon & Schuster, New York.

Chomsky, N. (2016a). Who rules the world, Hamish Hamilton, London.

Chomsky, N. (2016b). Profit over people: War against people, Piper, Berlin.

Christensen, C.M. (2016). The Clayton M. Christensen reader, Harvard Business School Press, Boston, MA.

Coates, K.S. & Morrison, B. (2016). Dream factories, Dundum, London.

Dorling, D. (2015). Inequality and the 1%, Verso, London.

Enderwick, P. (ed.) (1989). Multinational service firms, Routledge, London.

Evans, D.S. & Schmalensee, R. (2016). Matchmakers, Harvard Business Review Press, Boston, MA.

Fairtlough, G. (2007). Three ways of getting things done: Hierarchy, heterarchy and responsible autonomy in organizations, Triarchy Press, New York.

Fisher, J.D. (2006). The dynamic effects of neutral and investment-specific technology shocks, Journal of Political Economy, 114, 3: 413–451.

Ford, M. (2016). The rise of the robots: Technology and the threat of mass unemployment, One-World, London.

Foster, P.A. (2014). The open organization, Gower, New York.

Frey, C.B. & Osborne, M.A. (2013). The future of employment: How susceptible are jobs to computerization, Oxford Martin School Press, Oxford.

Gans, J. (2016). The disruption dilemma, The MIT Press, Boston, MA.

Garud, R., Kumaraswamy, A. & Langlois, R. (2002). Managing in the modular age: New perspectives on architectures, networks and organizations, Wiley-Blackwell, New York.

Garza, D. (2013). Disrupting, Create Space, New York.

Gaskarth, J. (ed.) (2015). China, India and the future of international society, Rowman & Littlefield, London.

Gershuny, J. & Fisher, K. (2014a). Post-industrious society: Why work time will not disappear for our grandchildren, Centre for Time Use Research, Department of Sociology, University of Oxford.

Gershuny, J. & Fisher, K. (2014b). Post-industrious society: Why work time will not disappear for our grandchildren, Centre for Time Use Research, Department of Sociology, University of Oxford.

Gollan, P.J. (2010). Employer strategies towards non-union collective voice, in Wilkinson, A., Gollan, P.J., Marchington, M. & Lewin, D. (eds). The Oxford handbook of participation in organizations, Oxford University Press, Oxford, pp. 212–236.

Goodman, J. (2015). Crisis, movement, management: Globalising dynamics, Routledge, London.

Gratton, L. (2011). The shift, Collins, London.

Gupta, S., Habjan, J. & Tutek, H. (2016). Academic labour unemployment and global higher education: Neoliberal politics of funding and management, Palgrave, London.

Gutmann, A. & Thompson, D. (1996). Democracy and disagreement, Harvard University Press, Cambridge, MA.

Hamel, G. (2008). Introduction, in Skarzynski, P. & Gibson, R. (eds). Innovation to the core, Harvard Business Press, Boston, MA, pp. xvii–xix.

Hamel, G. (2012). What matters now, Jossey-Bass, New York.

Hislop, D. (2013). Knowledge management in organizations, Oxford University Press, Oxford.

Hlupic, W. (2014). The management shift, Palgrave MacMillan, New York.

Johannessen, J.-A. (2016b). Systemic thinking, Volume 1: Aspects of the Philosophy of Mario Bunge, Create Space, New York.

Johnson, M. (ed.) (2015). Precariat: Labour, work and politics, Routledge, London.

Kessler, S. (2017). Gigged: The end of jobs and the future of work, Random House Business, New York.

Kiggins, R. (2017). The political economy of robots, Palgrave, London.

Lima, P.U. (2017). Autonomous mobile robotics: A system perspective, CRS Press, New York.

Mason, P. (2015). Post capitalism: A guide to our future, Allen Lane, London.

McAffee, A. & Brynjolfsson, E. (2017). Machine platform: Harnesing the digital revolution, W.W. Norton Company, New York.

Meister, J.C. & Mulcahy, K.J. (2017). The future workplace experience, McGraw Hill, New York.

Noonan, N.C. & Nadkarny, V. (2016). Challenge and change, Palgrave, London.

Piketty, T. (2016). Chronicles: On our troubled times, Viking, London.

Pink, D. (2001). Free agent nation, the future of working for yourself, Grand Central Publishing, New York.

Ramaswamy, V. & Ozcan, K. (2014). The co-creation paradigm, Stanford University Press, Stanford, CA.

Robertson, B.J. (2015). Holocracy: The revolutionary management system that abolishes hierarchy, Penguin, London.

Ross, A. (2016). The industries of the future, Simon & Schuster, London.

Sassen, S. (2015). The global city: New York, London, Tokyo, Princeton University Press, Princeton, NJ.

Schwab, K. (2016). The fourth industrial revolution, World Economic Forum, Geneva.

Sennett, R. (2006). The culture of the new capitalism, Yale University Press, London.

Sennett, R. (2009). The craftsman, Penguin, New York.

Sennett, R. (2013a). Together, Penguin, New York.

Sennett, R. (2013b). The rituals, pleasures and politics of cooperation, Penguin, London.

Shipler, D. (2005). The working poor, Vintage, New York.

Srinivasa, R. (2017). Whose global village?: Rethinking how technology shapes the world, New York University Press, London.

Standing, G. (2014a). The precariat: The new dangerous class, Bloomsbury Academic, New York.

Standing, G. (2014b). A precariat charter, Bloomsbury, London.

Stanford, M. (2013). Organization design: Engaging with change, Routledge, London.

Stearns, P.N. (2013). The industrial revolution in world history, Westview Press, New York.

Susskind, R. & Susskind, D. (2015). The future of professions: How technology will transform the work of human experts, Oxford University Press, Oxford.

Thurow, L. (1999). Creating wealth, Nicolas Brealey, London.

Wiedemer, D., Wiedemer, R.A. & Spitzer, C.S. (2015). Aftershock, Wiley, London.

Wilkin, S. (2016). Wealth secrets of the 1%: The truth about money, markets and multi-millionaires, Sceptre, London.

Wilson, M. (2017). Implementation of robot systems, Butterworth-Heinemann, New York.

Winfield, A. (2012). Robotics, Oxford University Press, Oxford.

Xie, S. (2017). Advanced robotics for medical rehabilitation, Springer, London.

Zhao, J., Feng, Z., Chu, F. & Ma, N. (2017). Advanced theory of constraint and motion analysis for robot mechanisms, Academic Press, London.

3 Innovation and the future of work

Introduction

Any social system that fails to balance stability and change, and at the same time be innovative, will not be able to steer the ship at a time of increasing complexity (Brynjolfsson & McAfee, 2014; Christensen, 2016). Postponing restructuring to prevent social consequences can be compared with an alcoholic trying to cure his hangover by 'a hair of the dog' strategy (i.e. taking another drink); such a strategy inevitably leads to the alcoholic 'falling off the wagon' (i.e. relapsing into alcoholism again). Similarly with social systems: the social consequences will only increase the more you employ this strategy. What one gains in time by postponing the consequences, one loses in energy, creativity, vitality and the long-term survival of the system (Hlupic, 2014; Goodman, 2015). The ability to change and innovate at the same time as maintaining stability is the test that any viable social system must undergo during the transition to the Fourth Industrial Revolution (Schwab, 2016).

At a general level, several authors have identified three features of the emergence of the information society (Machlup, 1962, 1981; Bell, 1971, 1979; Touraine, 1988; Toffler, 1990; Dordick & Wang, 1993; Drucker, 1999, 1999a; Thurow, 1999; Standing, 2014; Johnson, 2015):

1. **Competence and talent** will become an increasingly important factor for productivity;
2. **The service sector** will become the dominant source of employment;
3. **Freelancers** will comprise a key element of the employment structure.

These three features will bring extreme specialization and cascades of innovations to the front of the information economy.

The point that the service sector will be the dominant provider of employment does not mean that industrial production will be less significant in the Fourth Industrial Revolution. To the contrary, it will be very important, but not necessarily as a source of employment, either in long-established industrial nations or globally in newly established industrial centres, according to the robotization of the economy. Many jobs in the service and information/

knowledge sectors are in fact dependent on industrial production and linked to it in various ways (Cohen & Zysman, 1987; Bauman, 2011; Kiggins, 2017).

The transition to the Fourth Industrial Revolution changes the employment structure in all industries (Lima, 2017; Wilson, 2017). Consequently, wealth-creation processes are also changing, due to changes in organizational logic and new technology (Bennis et al., 2012; Xie, 2017). It is becoming increasingly difficult to define and delimit what constitutes commodity production and services production, e.g. consider the following list as an example: software production, video production, design of mobile phones, design of hi-fi systems, design of cars, biotech aquaculture, biotech agriculture, robot fishery, drone agriculture, etc. An essential point here is that the extent of information and knowledge is increasing, both as input and in the final product of wealth-creation processes (Brynjolfsson & McAfee, 2011; Gershuny & Fisher, 2014).

Important in this context is the fact that how we organize and manage information and knowledge resources has a direct impact on what knowledge we develop and have access to (Case, 2016). However, 'how knowledge behaves as an economic resource we do not yet fully understand. We need an economic theory that puts knowledge into the centre of the wealth producing process' (Drucker, 1993: 167).

Between 1920 and 1970 in the G7 countries, there was a clear decline in employment in agriculture, but relatively stable employment in the industrial sector (Castells, 2015). However, between 1970 and 2010, the trend was different with a reduction in industrial employment (Bratianu, 2015). At the start of the Fourth Industrial Revolution in the G7 countries, services, information and knowledge occupations constitute the major part of the workforce (Brockbank, 2013; Charnock & Starosta, 2016). In other words, there has been a transition from work-intensive to capital-intensive jobs at the end of the twentieth century. Now we see the transition from information- and knowledge-intensive jobs to an increasing demand for innovation-intensive jobs (Barrat, 2015; Bleuer et al., 2017).

The question we examine here is the following: 'Which factors influence wealth-creation processes in the emergence of the Fourth Industrial Revolution?'

The questions asked to answer the main question are:

1. How does extreme specialization constitute wealth-creation processes in the emergence of the Fourth Industrial Revolution?
2. How do the cascades of innovation constitute wealth-creation processes in the emergence of the Fourth Industrial Revolution?

The aim is to develop concepts and models that can be used when analysing organizational aspects in order to promote wealth-creating processes in the Fourth Industrial Revolution. The vision is to develop a conceptual basis for a new organizational logic in the Fourth Industrial Revolution.

Figure 3.1 summarizes the introduction and is also the way in which we have organized this chapter.

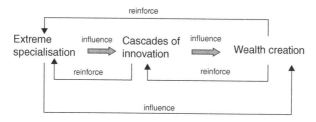

Figure 3.1 Wealth-creation processes in the Fourth Industrial Revolution.

Extreme specialization

Description

A particular feature of the information society is the global market for capital and competence. New technology makes the division of production, of both physical and virtual products, possible (Brynjolfsson & Saunders, 2013). One of the consequences of this division is that production and administration are outsourced globally and integrated into different types of global competence clusters (Brynjolfsson & McAfee, 2014). In this manner, the tendency towards extreme specialization is reinforced. Power is concentrated in a system of relations and a system of positions that are embedded in the different competence networks competing for attention (Case, 2016). These networks create the identities that are developed by people and organizations, and segment the market and exploit different niches in their habitats in order to survive (Fairtlough, 2007). The greatest levelling process will occur among these different networks, but there will also be a significant levelling process within each network (Castells, 2009, 2009a, 2015). Such a development may easily lead to a situation in which acceptance of greater differences becomes engrained in our way of thinking (Dorling, 2015).

When networks expand and monetary values take control of various domains, global power will take on an entirely different meaning (Wilkin, 2016). The global networks will gain greater control of national taxation policies, regional and investment policies, etc., because of the ease of moving capital and expertise in the global economy (Dickinson, 2016). If the networks are not comfortable with the regulatory frameworks, then they will merely 'flag out' to other global locations that can fulfil their requirements (Chomsky, 2012; McGill, 2016). The influence of the nation-state will thus be reduced in the Fourth Industrial Revolution (Case, 2016; Ford, 2016).

We always make observations on the basis of concepts and our experiences (Hamel, 2008: xvii–xix). Subsequently, we can say that truth is socially conditioned by the historical situation in which it occurs (Merton, 1967: 514). Against this background, it may be said that the experiences acquired by the global competence network in national contexts will establish guidelines for further action. Therefore, it becomes extremely important that the globalization of financial networks is met with a political network that is of at least the same calibre, so that the political context can provide the requisite variety (Ashby, 1961) to deal with the increasing complexity that arises.

Analysis and discussion

With their expertise and willingness to take the initiative and show commitment, the information and knowledge worker participates in the Fourth Industrial Revolution in various systems and competence networks (Coates & Morrison, 2016). From the businesses and networks in which they are active, they expect flexibility, autonomy, freedom and rewards based on delivered results (Drucker, 1999; Hamel, 2012). The new knowledge worker may be involved in various projects and criss-crossing networks, which may be partly in competition with each other (Drucker, 2005). The knowledge worker in such businesses and networks is, to an increasing extent, a free agent in relation to these conflicting interests. These free agents, or 'the company of one' (Lane, 2011) manages their own careers and flow of income. They create their own jobs within or outside a larger organization connected to a global network of expertise (Drucker, 1999a). The projects they generate are linked to competence, ambition and their private lifestyle (Florida, 2014). These free agents take part in projects and networks with more or less independent contracts for one or more systems. Their workplace may be home based, in a holiday cottage, their car, a tourist hotel, a tropical island, etc.; indeed, I personally know of someone who has their permanent 'work address' on cruise ships around the world. This is possible because the only thing they need is a computer and internet access. Cyberspace is their workplace (Dickinson, 2016). The working hours of this new knowledge worker are similar to those of the part-time project worker, although they participate in many different projects with different clients. Moreover, they work flexitime, in the real meaning of the word; flexibility is so great that new knowledge workers need to impose on themselves an almost neurotic work discipline, adapted to their own biorhythm (Goodman, 2015).

The new knowledge workers are the base units of the global networks. They often start their own businesses in connection with the organization(s) with which they have work relationships, and by their initiatives can change the direction of the whole of the established network. In this situation, the assumption is that knowledge workers feel that they gain something from the initiative in some way: independence, self-actualization, symbolic distinctions and a high degree of vanity are their driving forces (Florida, 2014). They are not hemmed in by trying to climb bureaucratic ladders or positioning themselves in traditional hierarchical power structures (Mason, 2015). They are guided by themes, problems, phenomena and challenges, and have little or no loyalty to or identity with the organization that happens to pay their salary. Their identity is related to problem and thematic areas.

The 'good life' is a basic foundation for these people, although what constitutes the good life varies for different knowledge workers. One thing that seems to be common to many of them is that wages in one form or another are an important mechanism that can enable them to attain the necessary freedom to develop their own version of the good life. They do not work to live, their work is their life and their hobby, and therefore the good life is related to their everyday work routines, not a strategy aimed at the 'good life' in retirement (Gollan, 2010; Jemielniak, 2014). They are effectively already 'retired' while they're working, because they can do their jobs as if it were their 'pastime'. They are what one might call the 'golf-playing workers', only they play golf while they are working. Leisure time is also their 'business time' (Gollan, 2010; Hanson, 2016). The characteristics that come out of this analysis are the self-centred, dynamic, ego-oriented, yet rational, solidarity-focused person, i.e. solidarity focused in so much as it serves their own interests. This analysis is an interpretation of research on the subject by Richard Sennett (1999, 2003, 2006, 2009, 2013), among others.

When businesses experience a growing recruitment problem, the first to jump ship are precisely those knowledge workers the business does not want to lose, because they are the most attractive in an expanding market. A strategy for retaining these workers will not necessarily be to offer them a market wage, but be related to what the individuals define as the good life for themselves. For instance, it may be the opportunity to work as free agents in relation to the organization, or depend on specific ways of working, or the opportunity of giving them access to exclusive networking, etc. One consequence of the new extreme specialization in the Fourth Industrial Revolution is that more knowledge workers will be carrying out tasks for several organizations, linked to different networks, in which small, tightly packed, social networks constitute the basic unit (Foster, 2014). Knowledge and service workers of various types will, to an ever greater extent, be engaged on a project basis, which, among other things, may lead to control over their own time being more meaningful (Florida, 2014).

At the organizational level, the whole will be subdivided into smaller viable systems that operate independently, while serving the networks of which they are a part (Gershuny & Fisher, 2014). This complexity means that individual less-viable systems, which previously functioned as units, functions, processes and activities in the classic hierarchy, now operate as autonomous units in a complementary logic (Gupta et al., 2016). This logic may be named information management meta-design, as shown in Figure 3.2. Each of the units in Figure 3.2 is viable in the sense that it is part of a network that compiles the parts into a functioning whole (Niland et al., 1994; Lima, 2017). An essential purpose of extreme specialization is that the individual modules focus on executing narrow functions (Roat, 2016). The system of these modules in Figure 3.2 operating in a network ensures the requirements of generalization, and thus promotes context competence (Global Wealth Report, 2015). In this way, extreme specialization protects both in-depth expertise through specialization and breadth expertise through development of contextual knowledge, i.e. being able to understand the part and the whole perspective of interaction and coherence (Johannessen, 2016a). This part–whole competence that extreme specialization promotes, through the information management meta-design principles in Figure 3.2, helps

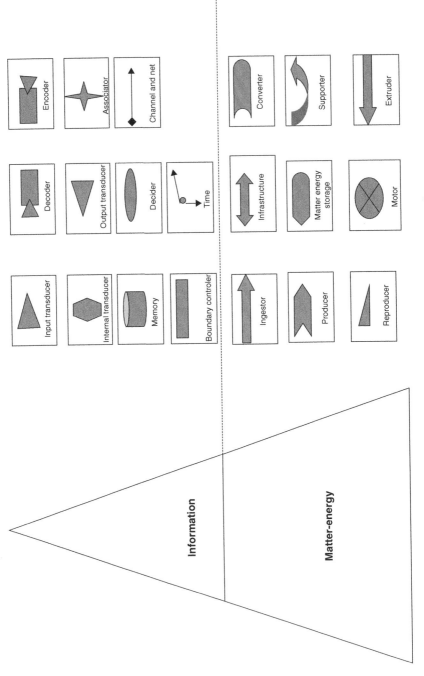

Figure 3.2 Information management meta design-functions as a consequence of extreme specialization.

to lay the ground for pattern understanding. It also helps to promote competition and cooperation within and between networks in the Fourth Industrial Revolution.

Organizing and leadership in extreme specialization are coordinated in a web-like structure of mediators, in which control impulses are determined by the system of relationships and positions in other networks (Monbiot, 2016). The mediating activity flourishes in such an organizational logic, where cost and quality focus are strong, because the individual units do not directly transfer competence from other units in the network, but must develop survival strategies based on connections to larger and expanding networks on a global basis (Noonan & Nadkarny, 2016). This will require mediators with the necessary part–whole understanding, i.e. the understanding of information management meta-design functions (see Figure 3.2). This will lead to a contextual and relational competence that connects the parts on a global basis to a functioning system for a specific time-limited activity (Organisation for Economic Co-operation and Development or OECD, 2014). A very clear consequence of this development is that employment conditions will be revolutionized in this new information management meta-design structuring of the global economy (Petras & Veltmeyr, 2011; Petras et al., 2013).

In the Fourth Industrial Revolution, manufacturing processes will also change significantly. The robotization of the production workers' and knowledge and service workers' activities will be necessary to increase productivity (Rojecki, 2016). Robotization will lead to production workers distancing themselves from production and working through automations, computers, informats[1] and various intermediate technological networks. In turn, informatization will lead to hierarchies turning in new directions, so that the frontline[2] comes into focus. One consequence of this development is that bureaucratization and control functions will be reduced and often removed, or replaced by informats and robots (Xie, 2017; Zhao et al., 2017). Informatization leads further to what we metaphorically may term 'robotic control'. This refers to small nano-computers found in physical objects that are connected to global networks (Abd, 2017; Wilson, 2017). Production, distribution, coordination and integration processes are robotically connected via various networks shaping the coming of informats (Frankish, 2014; Jemielniak, 2012). Digitalization and informatization also mean that the administrative information processes will be performed robotically through computer-like informats connected in a tightly structured global network (Lima, 2017).

The informats and robots may be of various types that access their computing power from the network, which is strengthened by connections to other informats and robots, i.e. the development of the global brain. Consequently, the capacity of the individual physical computers is not of interest; the interconnected robots are emerging into informats (Wilson, 2017; Zhao et al., 2017).

A social consequence of this development is that fewer people will have insight into the part–whole knowledge. The individual elements will conceivably be spread in the global network. In Figure 3.2, we included 20 functions and processes, which theoretically could be spread across the globe; however, all the functions and processes must be present for a specific product or service to be delivered (Miller, 1978).[3] In such a situation, the classic management and control mechanisms will change and possibly disappear to be replaced by new ones (Stanford, 2013; Foster, 2014; Goodman, 2015).

Sub-conclusion

The question asked was: 'How does extreme specialization constitute wealth-creation processes in the emergence of the Fourth Industrial Revolution?'

Extreme specialization leads to the rewriting of the social contract, and the social contract among businesses, workers and society will change dramatically in the Fourth Industrial Revolution.

Attributes such as creativity, commitment, adaptability, willingness to change, flexibility, friendliness, generosity and ability to innovate will all be in high demand. Extreme specialization and robotic control lead to the emergence of a new type of production, information, knowledge and service worker. One requirement for these will inevitably be an understanding of robots and informats, and an increasing degree of relational skills. This will require more abstract thinking,

Extreme specialization will enable production to be moved to areas around the globe where costs, expertise, creativity, innovation and quality are more optimal than in other areas. Extreme specialization in the Fourth Industrial Revolution will promote these developments, because it is extremely dependent on information and communication processes in technological networks.

Cascades of innovation and wealth creation

Description

'Ground Zero' for the information society is cascades of innovation changing the workplace and society. These changes will affect people in ways that may make them no longer feel that work is central to a sense of meaning in their lives (Standing, 2014). Already people feel less of a commitment to the jobs they already have.[4]

Technological development will lead to cascades of innovations (Hamel, 2008, 2012), which will affect economic growth, skills and expectations of the future in very different ways from what we have experienced previously, because the speed, feedback and distribution of ideas in the network will occur very quickly (Roat, 2016). Productivity will increase dramatically due to robotization, which will promote an exponential economic growth (Rodrik, 2011; Rosa & Mathys-Treio, 2015). However, wages will not necessarily follow productivity growth (Hanson, 2016).

Innovation cascades will occur with a rapidity not previously seen (Hanson, 2016; Noonan & Nadkarny, 2016), which will lead to minor and major economic staccato behaviour in the social system, because closures will be as common as innovation cascades. As a consequence, innovations will demolish established businesses and industries, which will be perceived as economic and social crises by those affected by these cascades (Johannessen, 2016). The labour market will change as rapidly as the innovation cascades enter the market (Hanson, 2016), with most jobs being experienced as unsafe, which will affect cohesion in the workplace and the role of trade unions (Rosa & Mathys-Treio, 2015; Bauman, 2013). When work is substituted by various types of robots, the traditional relationship between the employee and the purchaser of labour will change radically (Hanson, 2016; Sennett, 2013). In order to sell their expertise in this market, the simultaneous process of specialization and generalization will form a foundation for talent development, both on the individual level and in educational institutions (Pink, 2001; Charnock & Starosta, 2016).

In some instances, 'Ground Zero' in the information society concerns a transition from areas with heavy industry, such as the iron and steel industry, to areas of high technology (Petras et al., 2013; Sennett, 2013). The location of heavy industry usually depended on energy supply, whereas the location of high-tech industry depends on talent supply. One example of this 'Ground Zero' effect in the knowledge economy is Youngstown, Ohio, in the so-called Rust Belt. The town grew up on the steel industry, but, after bankruptcies, outsourcing and competition from India and China, Youngstown became a ghost town almost overnight. However, today in Youngstown, and in other steel and coal towns in, for example, the Ruhr area in Germany, a belt of high-technology businesses has sprung up. It is these high-tech businesses that symbolize development in the Fourth Industrial Revolution (Mason, 2015; Meister & Mulcahy, 2017).

Those who manage to adapt to the cascades of innovations from this 'Ground Zero' are thus winners in the information society (Wacquant, 2007, 2009; Swider, 2015). Those of the knowledge workers who don't manage to adapt will be the unemployed knowledge workers, who are often people with relatively long university educations, either Bachelor's or Master's degrees, but who are unable to find employment after they have completed their education (Coates & Morrison, 2016).

Young people who have only Bachelor's degrees are the future 'industrial workers'. Those students who have vocational Bachelor's degrees may be likened to skilled workers in industrial society. However, those students who have a general Bachelor's education that isn't professionally or vocationally oriented may be likened to unskilled workers in industrial society (Coates & Morrison, 2016; Dickinson, 2016). This means that knowledge and work are no longer interconnected, and a good university education is no longer any guarantee of permanent employment (Gupta et al., 2016).

Inequality appears to increase at an exponential speed in the information society, represented by the Fourth Industrial Revolution (Piketty, 2014, 2016; McGill, 2016). Solidarity in the workplace and the labour collective, which characterized the Second and sometimes the Third Industrial Revolutions, will be replaced by individual contract workers selling their labour like hirelings in the Middle Ages (Wacquant, 2009a; Sennett, 2013). The competition for jobs will increase the pushing down of wages, even if productivity increases (Bauman, 2013; Sprague, 2014). The community of workers in the traditional working class will be replaced by contract workers, freelancers, voluntary enterprises, entrepreneurs, project workers, 'the company of one', etc. (Gupta et al., 2016; Srinivasa, 2017). Robots, informats, artificial intelligence (AI) and the new nano-computers, systemically connected in a global network, will take over much of the work activities.

Analysis and discussion

Cascades of innovations will lead to constant disruptions in the way we work (Sennett, 2013), creating new winners and losers, affecting our relationships and not least our expectations for the future (Hanson, 2016). Uncertainty will become the norm, whereas inequality will be a necessary condition for society's cohesion and development (Bauman, 2013; Piketty, 2016).

Global organizations will steer the development of nations (Case, 2016), which must find new ways of defining democracy in order to take part in the emerging feudal capitalism of the Fourth Industrial Revolution. Feudal structures will be developed not only at an organizational level but also at a national level (Mason, 2015; Dickinson, 2016; McGill, 2016). According to both Hanson (2016) and Rosa and Mathys-Treio (2015), the great changes in people's lives, both in the present and in their expectations of the future, will lead to a revolt against national governing authorities. The time between when people 'have had enough' and when the authorities intervene to implement changes will increasingly become less (Savage, 2015). On the other hand, disgruntled individuals will connect to new technological platforms so that discontent will spread rapidly (Case, 2016). The time for the authorities to analyse, discuss and reflect issues will be reduced, and result in a staccato-type behaviour, and ad-hoc communities will most probably develop (Sennett, 2013; Bauman, 2013). Against this background, democracy may be reformulated to stability through feudal structures, a form of democracy, through bank committees (Wacquant, 2009, 2009a).

If the above analysis is correct then rapidity linked to Ashby's law of requisite variety (Ashby, 1961) will develop. This means that the authorities will always have the necessary resources to intervene against any dissatisfaction that may surface.

The necessary prerequisite for achieving this is a powerful and extensive bureaucracy. The power asymmetry may easily lead to further enhancement of conflicts between citizens and governments. In this way, the bureaucracy will function as a shackle on democracy, because citizens will easily associate democracy with the bureaucracy, and thus react against democracy, wanting something different, something stable and predictable. In this case, feudal structures may be the solution for the authorities, if not for democracy. The circle will thus be complete. The Fourth Industrial Revolution will promote a form of feudal capitalism and a feudal state structure. Employees will be the new hirelings in such a structure (Petras et al., 2013; Wiedemer et al., 2015; Roat, 2016).

The cascades of innovations in the Fourth Industrial Revolution will dominate; they will govern the development of all structures. Although the desire for stability and predictability will be prominent, this desire may be overridden by cascades of innovation and their destructive forces at all levels: the individual, organizational and national.

Dynamic collaborative networks among people, institutions, regions, countries and groups of countries will be an important driver of the information economy in its early stages (Castells, 2009, 2015). This also means that national boundaries will be of less importance than before. On the other hand, how they act to facilitate their participation in this development will be important for the integration of individual states into the global economy. This is thus a two-sided process in which development, on the one hand, is driven by forces that the nation state has no control over, whereas, on the other, the nation state's involvement will be very important in relation to how various collaborative networks connect the national state to the global economy (Chomsky, 2012; Charnock & Starosta, 2016).

Concentration in various types of innovative environments appears to be a social mechanism behind both dynamic collaborative networks and loose social organizations that promote innovation and wealth creation, and rebellion against the distribution of wealth creation (Castells, 2015; McGill, 2016).

The development of innovative environments is a task for established institutions, such as universities, colleges, authorities of various kinds or other institutions with good organizational skills. However, an important mechanism is also to create loose connections to new innovators, allowing offshoots and new branches to develop without established institutions managing the processes. In this way, internal dynamics will be created, attracting the necessary skills, investments and interest from a market. When this happens investments in the new emerging innovations will lead to flocking behaviour; everyone will have a bit of the pie. This flocking behaviour leads in the end to bubbles bursting, and when this happens it leads to minor and major economic and social crises (Figure 3.3).

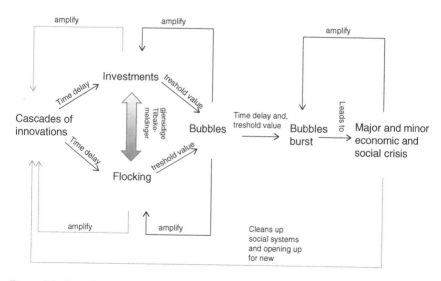

Figure 3.3 Cascades of innovation lead to minor and major economic and social crises.

Sub-conclusion

The question asked was: 'How does cascades of innovation constitute wealth-creation processes in the emergence of the Fourth Industrial Revolution?' The short answer is that cascades of innovation create wealth by destructing the old wealth-creation processes at the same time as creating the new processes. When this happens, cascades of innovation create creative destruction at all levels, individual, organizational and societal. In the end disruption cleans up social systems and opens up new cascades of innovations, so the circle repeats itself.

Conclusion

The question we have investigated in this chapter is: 'Which factors influence wealth-creation processes in the emergence of the Fourth Industrial Revolution?' Below, we suggest some tentative syntheses in response to this research question.

Robots, nano-computers and informats will interact with each other, permeating all areas of employment; figuratively, this could be imagined as neurons interacting in the human brain (see Figure 3.2). Familiarity with contexts and the direct 'hands-on' contact required by traditional industrial production will be given less emphasis, which will have enormous implications for educational institutions, and their educational programmes and methods

The robots, nano-computers in networks and informats will be characterized by a tripartite organization. First, the market will be developed for robot operators who will not need background knowledge other than experience in the work they perform, i.e. they are skilled production workers and will receive the appropriate training. Second, the traditional knowledge professions will be developed by reinforcing their knowledge base in relation to the design and development of the informats. Third, new disciplines and professions will be developed that design, develop and maintain robotic machines, informats and nano-computers.

This tripartite division will revolutionize the education market at all levels and, at the same time, new symbolic distinctions will be created. In other words, new hierarchies will be developed based on symbolic divisions.

The Fourth Industrial Revolution will most likely replace the pyramid hierarchies. However, this must not be misunderstood as the development of greater power distribution and equality in the system; it just means that power will change character. It is probable that various types of structurally connected competence networks will emerge, in which the system of relationships and positions provides control impulses. At the same time, the integration of such networks will be based on a set of norms and values where rational solidarity reigns, i.e. one shows solidarity because one benefits from it.

The economy, the outlines of which we can detect in the Fourth Industrial Revolution, is global, innovative and, to a large extent, technology driven. This element of globalism and innovation suggests that the speed of future changes may transform social systems worldwide in a rapid and brutal manner.

In the information economy, rapid economic upturns may rapidly transform to economic stagnation and downturns in specific geographical areas worldwide. In this kind of economy, innovation will be the most important competitive factor. Talent and expertise will become the social mechanism that triggers necessary social processes promoting extreme specialization and innovation. New technology, robotization and systemically connected nano-computers will promote information, communication and networking processes in and between businesses and systems of businesses. In this manner, time and distance will be eliminated around the globe with new technology.

The consequences of this will include an increasing rate of innovation and with it turbulence, the latter being augmented by the fact that global competence clusters will be working 24/7. These 24/7 networks will be the new mode of working.

In such an economy, it will not help to be the best at something within one's geographical area, because there will always be new arrivals who are better, more aggressive, and use unfamiliar and more ruthless methods of competition.

The main factor that influence wealth-creation processes in the emergence of the Fourth Industrial Revolution is cascades of innovation. The social mechanisms creating these cascades is extreme specialization. The chapter summarizes the answer to the following question: 'How can we know where the next innovations will emerge, so we can prepare a policy to hamper some of the consequences?' Figure 3.4 gives a response to this question.

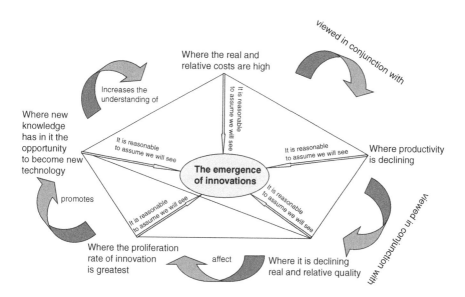

Figure 3.4 The emergence of innovations.

The social mechanism that is absolutely essential to drive these processes of creative destruction is the existence of people who are willing to take risks, and entrepreneurs who see opportunities for profit where others see problems and limitations. In such a situation, if we have a culture that limits processes of creative destruction, wealth creation will be significantly restricted. Wealth-creation processes in the new information economy require changes to be made to the structures that were necessary to the industrial economy, because the establishment has a tendency to want to uphold the status quo, and change always contains the potential for power shifts.

The development of a culture of entrepreneurship is essential for wealth creation in the knowledge economy, because competence and technology must be coupled to a willingness to take risks in order to provide opportunities for the new to emerge.

It appears that four criteria must be satisfied in order to build effective social mechanisms for wealth-creation systems in the Fourth Industrial Revolution:

1. Competitive educational systems;
2. Competitive infra- and infostructures;
3. Competitive research systems; and
4. Competitive entrepreneurship systems.

These four criteria should be investigated further in order to understand and apply in practice.

Notes

1 Informats are robots that are globally interconnected.
2 Those who work in direct interaction with the customer, patients, students, users, etc.
3 The 20 functions are derived from Miller (1978), but the symbols are obtained from Johannessen (1990).
4 Seventy per cent of those questioned in a large survey by Gallup in 2014 show a declining job satisfaction (*Information*, 22 June 2016).

References

Abd, K.K. (2017). Intelligent scheduling of robotic flexible assembly cells, Springer, London.

Ashby, W.R. (1961). An Introduction to Cybernetics, Chapman & Hall, New York.

Barrat, J. (2015). Our final invention, St Martin's Griffin, London.

Bauman, Z. (2011). Culture in a liquid modern world, Polity Press, London.

Bauman, Z. (2013). Does the richness of the few benefit us all? Polity, London.

Bell, D. (1971). Technocracy and politics, Survey, 16, 1–24.

Bell, D. (1979). The social framework of the information society, in Dertouzos, M. L. & Moses, J. (eds). The computer age: Twenty-year view, MIT Press, Cambridge, MA, pp. 163–211.

Bennis, W.G., Cloke, K. & Goldsmith, J. (2012). The end of management and the rise of organizational democracy, John Wiley & Sons, New York.

Bleuer, H., Bouri, M. & Mandada, F.C. (2017). New trends in medical and service robots, Springer, London.

Bratianu, C. (2015). Organizational knowledge dynamics, Information Science Reference, New York.

Brockbank, W. (2013). Overview and Logic. in Ulrich, D.; Brockbank, W.; Younger, J. & Ulrich, M. (eds). Global HR competencies: Mastering competitive value from the outside in, McGraw Hill, New York, pp.3–27.

Brynjolfsson, E. & McAfee, A. (2011). Race against the machine, Digital Frontier Press, New York.

Brynjolfsson, E. & McAfee, A. (2014). The second machine age, W.W. Norton & Company, New York.

Brynjolfsson, E. & Saunders, A. (2013). Wired for innovation: How information technology is reshaping the economy, The MIT Press, London.

Case, S. (2016). The third wave, Simon & Schuster, New York.

Castells, M. (2009). The power of identity, Wiley-Blackwell, Oxford.

Castells, M. (2009a). The rise of the network society, Wiley-Blackwell, Oxford.

Castells, M. (2015). Networks of outrage and hope, Polity Press, New York.

Charnock, G. & Starosta, G. (2016). The new international division of labour: Global transformation and uneven development, Palgrave, London.

Chomsky, N. (2012). How the world works, Hamish Hamilton, London.

Christensen, C.M. (2016). The Clayton M. Christensen reader, Harvard Business School Press, Boston, MA.

Coates, K.S. & Morrison, B. (2016). Dream factories, Dundum, London.

Cohen, S. & Zysman, J. (1987). Manufacturing matters: The myth of post-industrial economy, Basic Books, New York.

Dickinson, E. (2016). Globalization and migration, Rowman & Littlefield, London.

Dordick, H.S. & Wang, G. (1993). The information society: A retrospective view, Sage, New York.

Dorling, D. (2015). Inequality and the 1%, Verso, London.

Drucker, P. (1993). Post-capitalist society, butterworth, Heinemann, Oxford.

Drucker, P.F. (1999). Knowledge worker productivity: The biggest challenge, California Management Review, 41, 2: 79–94.

Drucker, P.F. (1999a). Management challenges for the 21st century, Harper Collins, New York.

Drucker, P.F. (2005). Managing oneself, Harvard Business Review, Jan. 100–109.

Fairtlough, G. (2007). Three ways of getting things done: Hierarchy, heterarchy and responsible autonomy in organizations, Triarchy Press, New York.

Florida, R. (2014). The rise of the creative class, Basic Books, New York.

Ford, M. (2016). The rise of the robots: Technology and the threat of mass unemployment, One-World, London.

Foster, P.A. (2014). The open organization, Gower, New York.

Frankish, K. (2014). The cambridge handbook of artificial intelligence, Cambridge University Press, Cambridge.

Gershuny, J. & Fisher, K. (2014). Post-industrous society: Why work time will not disappear for our grandchildren, Centre for Time Use Research, Department of Sociology, University of Oxford, Oxford.

Global Wealth Report (2015). http://publications.Credit-Suisse.com (Access date: 26 July 2016).

Gollan, P.J. (2010). Employer strategies towards non-union collective voice, in Wilkinson, A., Gollan, P.J., Marchington, M. & Lewin, D (eds). The Oxford handbook of participation in organizations, Oxford University Press, Oxford, pp.212–236.

Goodman, J. (2015). Crisis, movement, management: Globalising dynamics, Routledge, London.

Gupta, S., Habjan, J. & Tutek, H. (2016). Academic labour unemployment and global higher education: Neoliberal politics of funding and management, Palgrave, London.

Hamel, G. (2008). Introduction, in Skarzynski, P. & Gibson, R. Innovation to the core, Harvard Business Press, Boston, MA, pp.xvii–xix.

Hamel, G. (2012). What matters now, Jossey-Bass, New York.

Hanson, R. (2016). The age of Em: Work, love and life when robots rule the world, Oxford University Press, Oxford.

Hlupic, W. (2014). The management shift, Palgrave MacMillan, New York.

Jemielniak, D. (2012). The new knowledge workers, Edward Elgar, Cheltenham.

Jemielniak, D. (2014). The laws of the knowledge workplace, Gower, London.

Johannessen, J.-A. (1990). Information management, Stockholm University, Stockholm, PhD thesis.

Johannessen, J.-A. (2016). Innovations leads to economic crises, explaining the bubble economy, Palgrave, London.

Johannessen, J.-A. (2016a). Systemic thinking, Volume 1: Aspects of the philosophy of mario bunge, Create Space, New York.

Johnson, M. (eds). (2015). Precariat: Labour, work and politics, Routledge, London.

Kiggins, R. (2017). The political economy of robots, Palgrave, London.

Lane, C.M. (2011). A company of one: Insecurity, independence and the new world of white-collar unemployment, ILR Press, New York.

Lima, P.U. (2017). Autonomous mobile robotics: A system perspective, CRS Press, New York.

Machlup, F. (1962). The production and distribution of knowledge in the United States, Princeton University Press, Princeton, NJ.

Machlup, F. (1981). Knowledge and knowledge production, Princeton University Press, Princeton, NJ.

Mason, P. (2015). Post capitalism: A guide to our future, Allen Lane, London.

McGill, K. (2016). Global inequality, University of Toronto Press, Toronto.

Meister, J.C. & Mulcahy, K.J. (2017). The future workplace experience, McGraw Hill, New York.

Merton, R. (1967). On the history and systematics of sociological theory, in Merton, R.. (ed.). On theoretical sociology, The Free Press, New York, pp. 1–37.

Miller, J.G. (1978). Living Systems, McGraw-Hill, New York.

Monbiot, G. (2016). How did we get into this mess? Politics, equality, nature, Verso, London.

Niland, J.R., Lansbury, R.D. & Venevis, C. (ed.). (1994). The future of industrial relations. Sage, London.

Noonan, N.C. & Nadkarny, V. (2016). Challenge and change, Palgrave, London.

OECD. (2014). Policy challenges for the next 50 years, Brussels: OECD.

Petras, J. & Veltmeyr, H. (2011). Beyond neoliberalism: A world to win, Routledge, London.

Petras, J., Veltmeyr, H. & Marquez, H. (2013). Imperialism and capitalism in the twenty-first century: A system of crises, Routledge, London.

Piketty, T. (2014). Capital in the twenty-first century, The Belknap Press of Harvard University Press, Boston, MA.

Piketty, T. (2016). Chronicles: On our troubled times, Viking, London.

Pink, D. (2001). Free agent nation, the future of working for yourself, Grand Central Publishing, New York.

Roat, H. (2016). Capital and collusion: The political logic of global economic development, Princeton University Press, Princeton, NJ.

Rodrik, D. (2011). The globalization paradox, Oxford University Press, Oxford.

Rojecki, A. (2016). America and the politics of insecurity, John Hopkins University Press, New York.

Rosa, H. & Mathys-Treio, J. (2015). Social acceleration, Columbia University Press, New York.

Savage, M. (2015). Social class in the 21st century, Penguin, London.

Schwab, K. (2016). The fourth industrial revolution, World Economic Forum, Geneva.

Sennett, R. (1999). The corrosion of character, W.W. Norton, New York.

Sennett, R. (2003). The fall of public man, Penguin, New York.

Sennett, R. (2006). The culture of the new capitalism, Yale University Press, London.

Sennett, R. (2009). The craftsman, Penguin, New York.

Sennett, R. (2013). Together, Penguin, New York.

Sprague, S. (2014). What can labor productivity tell us about the US economy, US Bureau of Labor Statistics, Beyond the numbers, 3, 12: May.

Srinivasa, R. (2017). Whose global village?: Rethinking how technology shapes the world, New York University Press, London.

Standing, G. (2014). The precariat: The new dangerous class, Bloomsbury Academic, New York.

Stanford, M. (2013). Organization design: Engaging with change, Routledge, London.

Swider, S. (2015). Building China, informal work and the new, Ilr Press, London.

Thurow, L. (1999). Creating wealth, Nicolas Brealey, London.

Toffler, A. (1990). Powershift: Knowledge, wealth and violence at the edge of the 21st century, Bantam Books, New York.

Touraine, A. (1988). Return of the actor: Social theory in post-industrial society, University of Minnesota Press, Minneapolis, MI.

Wacquant, L. (2007). Urban outcast, Polity, London.

Wacquant, L. (2009). Punishing the poor, Duke University Press, London.

Wacquant, L. (2009a). Prisons of poverty, University of Minnesota Press, New York.

Wiedemer, D.; Wiedemer, R.A. & Spitzer, C.S. (2015). Aftershock, Wiley, London.

Wilkin, S. (2016). Wealth secrets of the 1%: The truth about money, markets and multi-millionaires, Sceptre, London.

Wilson, M. (2017). Implementation of robot systems, Butterworth-Heinemann, New York.

Xie, S. (2017). Advanced robotics for medical rehabilitation, Springer, London.

Zhao, J., Feng, Z., Chu, F. & Ma, N. (2017). Advanced theory of constraint and motion analysis for robot mechanisms, Academic Press, London.

4　Powershift in the Fourth Industrial Revolution

Introduction

We are experiencing a new trend in organizational logic that has two aspects. On the one hand, the spirit of entrepreneurship seems to becoming an international role model (Cao et al., 2010) and, on the other, well-established businesses are currently undergoing significant restructuring with major social consequences (Garud et al., 2002; Barrat, 2015). This restructuring is not a new phenomenon. What is new, however, is the unaccustomed speed and ability for focusing on global information processes, robots, artificial intelligence (AI), digitalization and demands for return on capital in this recent restructuring (Carayannopoulos, 2009; Case, 2016).

Simultaneously, this is used as an argument for the necessity to maintain productivity and competitiveness. Organizations must be profitable enough to compete for investment capital, short-term speculative capital and long-term working capital (Frey & Osborne, 2013; Brynjolfsson & McAfee, 2014). When ever more people invest their savings in funds of various types, they expect a higher rate of return than keeping money in the bank. Consequently, investors demand higher returns. In order to achieve this, there is a focus on costs and innovation in businesses, and the social systems surrounding these businesses. This leads to an increasing focus on what the system is designed to do, and thus a separation from those processes that do not directly support the business's main concept. The result is new ways of working and an emergence of a powershift in the Fourth Industrial Revolution (Schwab, 2016). In addition, although some businesses may be making a profit they are nevertheless 'wound down', because there are greater profits to be had by moving them to low-cost countries. At the same time, the focus is oriented towards new ideas, innovation and creativity, both within established companies and in start-up businesses. This processes leads to urbanization into cities and mega-cities[1] (Graham, 1994), and in these cities the new innovation centres of the fabric of knowledge are drawn towards the urban centre (Graham, 1994; Graham & Marvin, 1996; Pelling & Blackburn, 2013), where the innovation centres of the cities are often found (Mieg & Tøpfer, 2013; Denis & Zérah, 2017). We call this ICN-logic (information, communication and network logic).

The main question in this chapter is: 'Which factors leads to a powershift in the Fourth Industrial Revolution?'

In order to answer the main question we have developed three sub-questions:

Question 1: Which magnitudes are aspects of a powershift in the Fourth Industrial Revolution?

Question 2: How do new ways of working lead to a powershift in the Fourth Industrial Revolution?

Question 3: How does ICN-logic lead to a powershift in the Fourth Industrial Revolution?

Figure 4.1 summarizes this introduction and also demonstrates the ways in which this chapter is organized.

Powershifts in the Fourth Industrial Revolution

In this section, we describe, analyse and discuss which magnitudes are aspects of a powershift in the Fourth Industrial Revolution.

Description

A new organizational logic will be developed in the Fourth Industrial Revolution, not because of a predominantly more advanced moral or ethical approach, but because global competition has put the focus on competence, innovation and technology (Bratianu, 2015; Abd, 2017). Individual activities will be divided into systemic modules which will then be distributed globally according to a cost-, quality-, innovation- and competence-based logic (Abd, 2017; Wilson, 2017). Time spent meaningfully and geographical freedom will create the necessary preconditions for creativity and innovation (Brynjolfsson & McAfee, 2011; Brynjolfsson & Saunders, 2013). This is because people work most creatively when time is experienced as meaningful and, when one is free to work remotely, one will have entered organizational and senior management agendas at the dawn of the Fourth Industrial Revolution (Hamel, 2008, 2012).

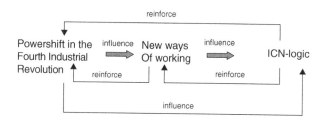

Figure 4.1 Powershift in the Fourth Industrial Revolution.

The motives for the changes mentioned above may vary, but what we should be aware of is the fact that the new organizational logic is not driven by consideration of people at the frontline. Rather meaningful time, the free choice of geographical location, and the growing demand for expertise and understanding of technology linked to networks will be important resources in the new wealth-creation processes (Noonan & Nadkarny, 2016).

The fact that morality, values and norms are put on the agenda in this process does not soften the face of power (Chomsky, 2016a). Rather, it is only the mask of power that changes, expressing itself in the network as a system of relationships and positions (Chomsky, 2016b). Power assumes the mask of norms and values, and is therefore difficult to ascertain (Armano & Murgia, 2015; Dorling, 2015).

Analysis and discussion

In the Fourth Industrial Revolution, the value chain will, to a greater extent than today, consist of the global competence network of more or less independent, autonomous, but systemically linked, suppliers (Barrat, 2015; Case, 2016; Abd, 2017). These systemically linked suppliers will undertake various activities depending on their expertise, technology and prevailing cost structures in the geographical areas.

The social processes that are triggered, maintained and changed in the Fourth Industrial Revolution can be understood as:

- The power of distribution of meaningful time (Chang, 2008);
- The power to organize the freedom of geographical location (Charnock & Starosta, 2016);
- The power to distribute positions (Coates & Morrison, 2016);
- The power to include and exclude (Dickinson, 2016);
- The power to control definitions (definition power) (Evans & Schmalensee, 2016);
- The power to define models (model power) (Chomsky, 2016a, 2016b).

The dynamic networks that make up the organizational logic of the information society are loosely connected to the various social networks, and strongly connected to the coordination and integration functions in various networks (Sennett, 2006, 2009; Bauman, 2011). The latter promotes information and communication flow, and the former prevents intermingling of the private and public spheres (Sennett, 2013).

Robotics, nano-computers and AI, as well as modular production design, enable wealth-creation processes based on meaningful time and freedom in terms of geographical location, i.e. remote working (Wilson, 2017; Zhao et al., 2017).

In the same way that hydropower was a localization factor for some of the first industrial processes, and to some extent still is, information and communication networks will have the same localizing effect in the Fourth Industrial Revolution (Brynjolfsson & Saunders, 2013; Brynjolfsson & McAfee, 2014). Similar to how hydropower structured the organization of work processes, the new organizational logic determines new localization patterns and new wealth-creation processes.

As mentioned above, from a polis perspective, the new technology may be imagined as having a dual impact on wealth-creation processes. Activity will be concentrated around city centres, where a substantial portion of knowledge processes takes place (Abrahamson, 2004). Knowledge and service occupations will increase the most in urban areas (Sanseverino & Sanseverino, 2017).

The powershift logic leads to a concentration of power and decentralization of creativity and innovation processes. The powershift is concentrated in the financial centres (Budd & Whimster, 1992; Chang, 2008; Chomsky, 2012).

Although some knowledge workers may have creative and fulfilling tasks, it shouldn't be assumed that this will be the case for service workers or unskilled workers. Nor will it be the case that decision-making about what to produce, where it should be produced, how surplus should be distributed, etc. will be localized to the same areas that develop the creative ideas. On the contrary, modular flexibility based on a new fragmentation of production will develop globally (Chandraekaren et al., 2012). From such a perspective, the knowledge economy is not significantly different from the industrial economy. The power élite has now rather adopted a new geographical space for its activities, so the powershift is therefore a transition from the local to the global scene and the world has become a single market where the local has become global, with regard to both production and consumption, with all the social, economic, cultural and political implications that this entails (Rodrik, 2011). Decision-making processes, power and decision-making authority still lie in the systems of positions and relationships (Castells, 2009, 2016). An empirical review of this concentration of power around the financial markets may be found in Budd and Whimster (1992) and Sassen (1991).

A significant feature of the new production processes is that they have been moved from specific locations to 'global space', i.e. the network takes over the integration and coordination functions (Castells, 2009a, 2009b, 2016). Production is modularized according to a cost, quality, innovation and competence logic. In practice, this means that the consumer and producer are in principle directly linked via the network. In this way, many of the intermediate functions in wealth-creation processes are eliminated. Management and control are done via the new technology. In the Fourth Industrial Revolution, highly trained technologists, professionals, research staff and individuals associated with the administrative professions are separated from both production and each other. The physical and social networks become the new coordinating elements in wealth-creation processes, and become the principal drivers of wealth creation.

When such a separation occurs, identities are developed based on different relationships than previously. These identities, based on the systems of relations and positions in social networks, will take on other forms to previously, because dependency is constantly changing. Instead of transparency and casting a critical light on social conditions, it may be in the interests of the dominant network to have opaque social processes and relationships, i.e. mask them to avoid clarification. This may be done by giving less emphasis to critical elements in the media, and giving the public more 'bread and circuses'. Of course, this assumes that the media are largely owned by the dominant social networks controlling production, distribution and sales (Castelfranchi, 2007).

In the industrial age, social inequalities were more visible, because everyone was more or less tied to a specific geographical location. Stratification was literally ordered along an east–west axis and the valley sides. Consumption was thus transparent. However, in the Fourth Industrial Revolution, although consumption is by no means less, on the contrary the differences and stratification are not visible to the same extent, because the network spans geographical distances, so the differences are less conspicuous. Inequalities are thus masked and visible only in statistics (McGill, 2016). The social differences are, metaphorically speaking, spread geographically along a global valley side, which largely follows the north–south axis of the planet, and to some extent also the east–west axis, with some exceptions (Henderson, 1989, 1990; Roat, 2016). This development started in the USA in the 1960s, and in Japan in the 1980s, says Castells (1989, 2016).

Figure 4.2 summarizes the power shifts in the Fourth Industrial Revolution.

Sub-conclusion

In this section we answered the question: 'Which magnitudes are aspects of powershift in the Fourth Industrial Revolution?' The short answer is the five magnitudes shown in Figure 4.2.

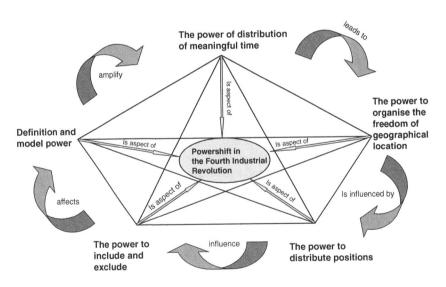

Figure 4.2 Powershift in the Fourth Industrial Revolution.

Theoretical and practical implications

The logic of capital in today's global world is such that everyone who invests their small savings helps to reinforce the urbanization processes. Consequently, we ourselves are responsible for the social consequences that are brought about through subtle structural couplings; paradoxically, we may later argue against these social consequences. The same logic is obviously applicable if we put our savings in various types of funds, or in roundabout ways borrow money from banks that profit from investing in such funds.

The point being made here is that we cannot blame an abstract concept such as globalization for the restructuring and the subsequent consequences that become evident globally. It is rather a part of the genetic code of capital's logic, regardless of the system, to ensure the system's survival. The logic of capital dictates that the survival of the total system takes precedence over the sub-system's survival; thus parts of the system often need to be laid waste for a period of time to achieve this. The total system thus 'cannibalizes' part of itself in order to survive and eventually improve its condition. The alternative to such cannibalization and creative destruction may be 'constant infection', to borrow a metaphor from medicine. If your body is constantly infected you will sooner or later be drained of energy, creativity and enthusiasm, and finally become completely dependent on others.

Globalization, strong structural connections, flexibility and the focus on costs drive economies towards urbanization, which in turn leads to production chains being broken up into modular flexible systems with an extreme customer focus. This leads to individual businesses orienting themselves towards the frontline, i.e. those businesses know what the customer wants and know how they can change production and service to increase customer satisfaction, and thus survive in a fierce, turbo economy, which is globalized and thus disconnected from local norms and values. Viewed from an organiza-tional perspective in individual organizations or networks of businesses, the strategy is thus modular flexibility and a frontline focus. It is these two elements that can affect the wealth creation processes in individual businesses in the most creative way, and result in the survival of social systems in the Fourth Industrial Revolution.

New ways of working

In this section we describe, analyse and discuss the question: 'How do new ways of working lead to a powershift in the Fourth Industrial Revolution?'

Description

When new ways of organizing work emerge, and robots take over many of the functions previously performed by middle-class workers, the administrative/ bureaucratic system will no longer enjoy the same legitimacy. None the less, it will continue to have great power (Avent, 2016). It is at this point of conflict that tensions may emerge (Barrat, 2015). When the work is no longer organized around the production of goods, but around the production of knowledge, new systems of governance will develop, and accordingly the legitimacy of the administrative/bureaucratic stratum will diminish (Bennis et al., 2012).

The fear of losing control over one's own life is an essential part of what we experience in the new workplace (Bolanski & Chiapello, 2017). The economic crisis that began in 2008 accelerated these concerns among many workers (Sennett, 2013). Therefore, willingness to change, be flexible and re-educate has become a constant factor for many workers (Ali, 2015). Part of the fear is also related to the fact that people's ethical values have become relative, i.e. they vary in relation to the external relationships they happen to have at any one time (Furnham, 1997; Pink, 2001). Among other things, this is related to an increasing tendency to change jobs more frequently; hence, lasting relationships are fewer and people's knowledge-base is changing more quickly than before (Standing, 2014a). Consequently, the time perspective is shifting from long term and stable to short term and temporary (Savage, 2015). Temporary jobs, whether on projects, contracts, part-time, as 'the company of one', etc., change the way people relate to others (Sennett, 2013; Sanseverino & Sanseverino, 2017). An indication of this development is the growth in employment agencies (Champy, 1995: 119; Standing, 2014b).

The fact that capital has changed character from being long term and patient to short term and impatient may provide one explanation of these temporary working relationships (Doeringer, 1991; Piketty, 2014). The short-term and impatient capital leads to a need for other, more easily soluble forms of organization. This may also partly explain the transition from hierarchical structures with their routines, bureaucracy with clear rules and greater predictability, to networks, where structures are often reconfigured very quickly (Wilkinson & Pickett, 2009; Rothkopf, 2012). However, although the new organizational logic may be partly explained by the new capital logic, it is made possible through the new technology.

Analysis and discussion

The willingness to change that leads to personal success will also correspond to the erosion of values, such as loyalty, trust, commitment, responsibility for others, etc. (Armstrong, 2014a, 2014b). In such a situation, these values may well be conserved as 'nostalgic' values from another time. On the other hand, it may well be that these values are given a second renaissance in small, tightly packed, social networks, whereas in looser, larger systems they will be given less emphasis (Sennett, 2006, 2009). If this happens, there is much to suggest that larger companies will feel compelled to reintroduce elements of the management and control measures associated with the early days of 'scientific management' (Srinivasa, 2017). However, in its consequences, such a development would only reinforce the collapse of close ties in organizations and de-emphasize loyalty, trust and responsibility for others (Bauman, 2011, 2013; Sennett, 2013).

Hyper-change and a high degree of flexibility lead to other types of control mechanisms coming into operation. The system of relationships and the networks of which they form a part becomes the essential control mechanisms, not the organizational hierarchy or bureaucratic regulatory management (Bennis et al., 2012). To achieve the desired flexibility most businesses will have to focus on their core activities, i.e. 'What is the system designed to do?' will become a key issue in the Fourth Industrial Revolution (Johannessen, 2016: 56). Thus, activities that are not directly focused on core activities will be given less emphasis or wound down. This will also result in hierarchical and bureaucratic control mechanisms being given less emphasis (Bratianu, 2015). This development could, however, easily lead to those who remain in the business developing dysfunctional behaviour, because they will be preparing to be the next to be 'put out in the woods to die', i.e. fall victim to cutbacks, etc. One may name this tendency the 'survival syndrome'.

It may often be the case, therefore, that survivors strategically position themselves in relation to such an expected future situation. This could become a self-fulfilling prophecy, because motivation and morale might conflict with management's expectations (Sennett, 2006). Such dysfunctional behaviour can also lead to negative consequences for production and productivity, which has been indicated by Applebaum and Batt (1993: 23) and Harrison (1994), as well as Harvey (2010) and Hlupic (2014).

Individual solutions will in turn promote the search for new identities, not what we stand for but rather what we represent. Demarcation from others will become more important when individual solutions win greater inroads, i.e. selling your individuality in a market. In such a world, how one presents oneself will become even more important, and we will see more people examining their mirrored reflections in an attempt to achieve 'the perfect' – in such a culture narcissism will have good days (Malkin, 2016). This may lead to greater respect being demanded for what one stands for, precisely because it is directly linked to one's survival in an increasingly competitive market. However, when assessments are not objective, it will be the one who can present their own subjective view effectively who prevails.

In this development, one can imagine that demonstrating solidarity with a particular class or strata of the population will be of lesser importance, precisely because one's own individuality and intellectual capital become an input factor in the market, regardless of affiliation.

There are many objections to such thinking. One is related to the large growth in service workers who sell their labour in a similar way to the industrial worker. Conversely, the industrial worker is better organized than the service worker, at least at present (Innerarity, 2012; Jemielniak, 2012). The low levels of organization will make it easier for employers to exploit negotiation advantages. The same may also be the case with the knowledge workers. Unless they hold critical key positions or cannot easily be replaced by other knowledge workers or robots, they will suffer the same fate as the service workers. The lack of organization of the knowledge workers may be used as a bargaining chip by employers in negotiations (Jiang et al., 2012).

Speed, flexibility and individual solutions also mean that mobility will increase, both within the individual's job situation and geographically (Hage & Powers, 1992; Godard, 2010). One consequence of this is that job insecurity for the individual will increase, which will affect the survival syndrome.

It may also be the case that in the Fourth Industrial Revolution risk-takers will have greater opportunities than those who are risk-averse (Mason, 2015; Meister & Mulcahy, 2017). The motivation and objective of risk-takers largely represent a kind of Eldorado: few get there, but those who do testify to the others about the possibilities and glory of being a risk-taker. It is therefore reasonable to assume that it is among the risk-takers that one will find the winners in the Fourth Industrial Revolution (Dickinson, 2016; Evans & Schmalensee, 2016). Simultaneously, this risk culture will drive forward greater inequality than we have so far seen in European welfare economies (Piketty, 2014; McGill, 2016).

When mobility increases, personal relationships are exposed to stress, which can easily result in Teflon relationships developing. The psychological contracts in which closeness and depth play a large role may be replaced by ephemeral and superficial relationships, in which functional solidarity becomes normal, i.e. solidarity is shown only to the extent it is useful to oneself (Sennett, 2006, 2013).

The superficial character of personal relationships will make it easier for individuals to create their own life story, because social ties will not hold a person back. Weak ties will thus be a strength for mobility both career-wise and geographically. One weakness of this strength is that the employee may find himself in a communicative vacuum. This means that the communication network that is the strength of close relationships will be eroded, and one will find oneself in the core of a communicative cyclone where tranquillity prevails (Sennett, 2013). A counter-strategy for the mobile nomad will be to be affiliated to a professional community, which ensures knowledge sharing that the communication network aims to maintain. Another strategy will be to actively use the new ICT to maintain personal relationships so that the communication network is kept intact. The point of this is that communication can, from a relational perspective, be more important than what is actually communicated. This means that communication as a symbolic act can have greater significance than the semantic content of communication.

Figure 4.3 summarizes how new ways of working will lead to a powershift in the Fourth Industrial Revolution.

Sub-conclusion

In this section we have answered the question: 'How do new ways of working lead to a powershift in the Fourth Industrial Revolution?' The short answer is the six factors in Figure 4.3.

Theoretical and practical implications

If network organization leads to short-sightedness in human relationships, then the obligation, commitment, trust and loyalty one has towards the organization

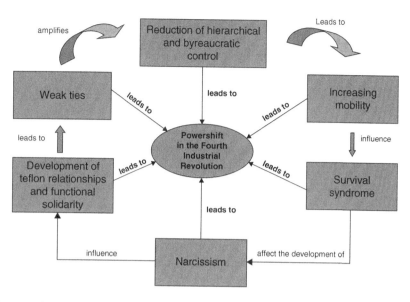

Figure 4.3 New ways of working leading to a powershift in the Fourth Industrial Revolution.

where one works will be transferred to one's self. This will enhance egocentrism and result in greater individualization. Such a development would lead to a fragmentation of social relationships. The superficial relationships we have indicated here may well prove to be a necessary condition for organizational flexibility. It is reasonable to think that less emphasis on relationships based on trust, binding commitment and loyalty will lead to more emphasis being placed on individuals taking responsibility for themselves. This will strengthen mobility, flexibility, narcissism, Teflon relationships, functional solidarity and the willingness to change. On the other hand, collective ties and norms will be emphasized less.

The personal crises resulting from such a transition to a new work logic will lead to individual solutions that will change values and basic norms in the workplace. Cuts, elimination of functions and departments that are moved to other entities, concentration on core processes and robots taking over functions will lead to increased turbulence, less emphasis on collective solutions and thus a greater emphasis on individual solutions. The acceptance of personal initiatives and individual solutions as a strategy for success, in contrast to the work collective, may appear to be a significant change in the basic norms of the workplace. Rapid changes in working life will be accepted as if they were natural laws, which are, per definition, something you adhere to. Uncertainty has become the norm and security nostalgia. It is in this situation that the free agent, contract worker, project worker, 'the company of one', the precariat and working for several employers will become rational individual solutions to the overarching changes in working life.

A natural consequence of this development will be changes to basic norms and ethical attitudes. At least this will apply to utility or practical ethics, if not the ethical values one pronounces verbally. However, practical ethical values will eventually become so different from the outspoken ones that the latter will gradually be modified to accommodate the discrepancy in order to mitigate psychological tension.

ICN-logic

In this section, we describe, analyse and discuss the question: 'How does ICN-logic lead to a powershift in the Fourth Industrial Revolution?'

Description

ICN-logic is driven by globalization, the new technology, innovation and culture (Certomá et al., 2017). The new forms of technology, robots, informats and AI will lead to new methods of production, distribution and consumption, which will in turn affect how work is organized (Abd, 2017; Zhao et al., 2017). How technology drives value creation has been demonstrated many times in recent research, e.g. Schwab (2016), Brynjolfsson & McAfee (2014) and Bleuer et al. (2017), to name just a few.

A consequence of the new technology is an even greater focus on communication as the foundation stone of organization and management (Wilson, 2017). Already in 1969, Karl E. Weick said that it is precisely communication that is the foundation stone of organization (Weick, 1979: 35). How we communicate, with whom, through what channels and with what effect are therefore entirely central to organizational logic. All communication takes place with the help of some form of symbols, which can be expressed by cave paintings or by electronic messages. Communication is understood as a reciprocal stream of messages in a network (Bateson, 1972: 399–410).

A message consists of three components: first, the information component is the message's core; second, it consists of a relational component, which concerns how to understand, interpret and perceive a message, and depends on the relationship you have with the sender, e.g. if the message were from one's wife, one would interpret it in one way, whereas, if it came from the tax authorities one would orient the interpretation on another frequency; and, third, the message is composed of a hierarchical component, which can have implications for interpretation, e.g. in a military context, one would interpret a message differently depending on whether it came from an equal, such as say Private Brown, or a superior, such as a colonel. All three components of a message are placed in a context that sends context markers to the receiver, who then interprets the message on the basis of this context. An essential point related to the organization of the message is how one is integrated into the communication processes that take place in the context or network of which one is a part.

Another point is whether you are the acting or reacting party in the network. If you are not integrated into the communication processes then you are outside the new organizational logic, because it is this ICN-logic that prevails in the new wealth-creation processes. If you do not have the opportunity to be the acting party in a network or system, then there are others who act on your behalf. However, this may be disadvantageous, because the motives of others need not be congruent with your own. The new emphasis on communication, through ICN-logic and network thinking, is an important driving force behind the Fourth Industrial Revolution (Schwab, 2016).

Analysis and discussion

The new technology connected to ICN-logic results in what may seem to be a paradoxical consequence. The paradox is that all assumptions point in the direction that people should be able to live a comfortable life in their familiar surroundings at any locality around the world using the new technology (Catmull, 2014). However, developments seem to point to the opposite tendency. People are moving to urban areas like never before, and especially to core centres in urban areas (Barrat, 2015). It would seem that communication promotes communication within the context of a polis logic (Sassen, 2002; Case, 2016).

'Polis logic' is of course as old as the concept is, about 2500 years old. In polis logic, people are concerned about the development in central urban areas. Also there is the polis logic that develops agora, i.e. meeting places in the polis where communication and innovation may be developed. Agora is driven by the need to create relationships and to participate in the stories that prevail in the network in question, and thus be part of the creative development of the Fourth Industrial Revolution (Catmull, 2014; Gupta et al., 2016).

Communication may then conceivably be imagined as taking place between the agoras in the various urban centres of various polises, such as Paris, London, New York and Tokyo. It may be said that these are more interconnected than the respective agoras are to the surrounding areas of these global cities. In this way, a stream of messages is developed, where technology, innovation and knowledge are created and disseminated. In the Fourth Industrial Revolution, this also creates 'backwaters', which are left behind during economic growth and wealth creation.

Agoras are the meeting places in the various polises where global, multi-cultural, private and public spaces meet, coordinate and integrate. In other words, the parts are woven together into a whole and a common meaning is generated precisely in these agora areas of the various polises. The size of the polis is not the defining characteristic of its existence. It is the system of relations (economic, political, cultural and social), both internally in the polis and between the polises, that characterizes the existence of the various agoras and polises.

For instance, the system of relations in polis and agora may be expressed as:

* Control over the media;
* Control of the formation of meaning;

- Control of the political agenda;
- Control over economic structures and processes;
- Control over political structures and processes;
- Control over cultural structures and processes.

Polis logic may easily result in isolating the population in rural areas, so they are symbolically excluded from the formation of meaning. They will be put in a position of reacting rather than acting in communication networks. This may eventually lead to a conflict among the polises, agoras and rural areas.

Polis logic will be at the centre of the cultural, economic, political, technological and social dynamics in the Fourth Industrial Revolution (Brynjolfsson and McAfee, 2011; Jemielniak, 2014). The polises and agoras will therefore act as magnets for the surrounding areas and further enhance this development. An indicator of how an area will evolve in relation to technology, innovation and knowledge may be related to the development of the polises and agoras in the geographical areas of interest for analysis.

At the global level, it is the large cities and metropolises that dominate knowledge development and supply knowledge to the private sector (Case, 2016; Bleuer et al., 2017). Polis logic displays another interesting phenomenon, namely that the ties between the various polises, e.g. urban areas in the EU, become stronger, whereas the ties between town and country become weaker. This has been shown to be the case in the EU by Cappelin (1991), and is mentioned by Case (2016) and Brynjolfsson and Saunders (2013).

Within the various levels of the network, i.e. the global, regional and national, this hierarchical logic of polises, agoras and rural areas will become clearer (Castells, 1989: 385; Dickinson, 2016). At the national level, this means that the various polises will become more important, whereas the opportunities in rural areas will largely depend on their connection to the polis areas, nationally, regionally or even to the global metropolises.

Metropolitan areas dominate in the field of knowledge development and the supply of knowledge to businesses (Sassen, 1991; Budd & Whimster, 1992; Rosa & Mathys-Treio, 2015). As mentioned above, metropolitan logistics display another interesting phenomenon, namely that the links between various large cities, e.g. metropolitan areas within the EU, become stronger and the relative links between 'town and country' become weaker. This has been demonstrated in the case of the EU by Cappelin (1991). These kinds of logistics will become ever more apparent in global, regional and national networks (Castells, 1989: 385; Catmull, 2014). At a national level, this will mean that the various metropolitan areas will gain increased significance, whereas opportunities for rural areas will to a large extent lie in forming connections with metropolitan areas, both nationally and regionally.

Figure 4.4 summarizes how ICN-logic will lead to a powershift in the Fourth Industrial Revolution in.

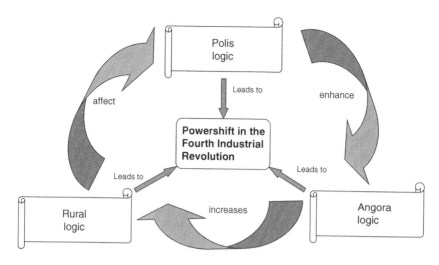

Figure 4.4 ICT-logic leading to a powershift in the Fourth Industrial Revolution.

Sub-conclusion

In this section we have answered the question: 'How does ICN-logic lead to a powershift in the Fourth Industrial Revolution? The short answer is that three magnitudes lead to the powershift initiated by ICN-logic: polis, agora and rural logic.

Theoretical and practical implications

Bypassing the national polices may be a very effective knowledge strategy for several of the smaller knowledge centres within a country. The rationale here relates to the historical mental models that often create psychological barriers in local areas. The 'left behind' psychology will always exist as a social obstacle, at least at the mental level in the system of relationships that constitutes a nation. It is only through network connections that the rural areas can be other than recreational areas for 'communication-tired' polis residents. In light of this understanding, one can delineate certain features of the Fourth Industrial Revolution's polis, agora and rural logic:

* Concentration of power in specific centres in the network;
* Increasing control over critical information and communication, and less control of information and communication that is not critical for the exercise of power;
* Stronger market specialization in certain systems, but also greater diversity in the context of networks, i.e. the simultaneous existence of specialization and diversity;

- The simultaneous existence of regulation and deregulation of barriers to trade, information, communication, labour, capital and knowledge processes;
- Increasing flexibility at all stages and levels in the various networks;
- Polis domination, economically, culturally, politically and relationally;
- The rural areas' resurgence as information mediators, e.g. in design, development of information products, suppliers of information and knowledge products;
- The production of goods and services will follow an extreme cost, quality and competence logic;
- The global dominance of the metropolises regarding management and control of trade and banking, as well as financial services.

Conclusion

The main question was: 'Which factors lead to a powershift in the Fourth Industrial Revolution?' The short answer is that six factors in the new ways of working, and three factors in the ICN-logic lead to a powershift in the Fourth Industrial Revolution.

Theoretical and practical implications

The urban areas, i.e. the various polises, will largely provide the framework for career development for young people. This will lead to new professions and career paths, which did not exist in the industrial era, becoming new high status occupations.

Educational level and knowledge will be important as a symbolic demarcation mechanism in the Fourth Industrial Revolution. In such a context, it seems reasonable that continuous skills development will be a factor that determines whether young people choose one career path over another. The expertise increasingly demanded by the knowledge society will occur in the polis areas. This implies a further concentration around the polis areas in the various regions.

The rural areas will become sub-suppliers of services and information to the polis areas, and centres of service and information processes will be developed. Where these centres are located will be of less importance; however, the choice of location will be subject to an extreme cost, quality, innovation and competence logic. To a large extent, competition will increase between the various rural areas of each country, and there will thus be as much tension between the rural areas as between the centre and periphery. Consequently, centralization and decentralization will exist simultaneously in a dynamic interplay in which speed and flexibility will be key elements.

The various systems of relationships and positions will constitute the networks' centres, where decisions are taken. However, these centres will not necessarily be geographically located. Power may be viewed as a process of the system of relationships that are developed in relation to certain activities and processes to perform specific tasks. Thus, the system of decision-making in the central networks will constitute the centres of power, not geographical locations.

Polis logic is largely driven by the social mechanisms that promote the development of innovative environments. These environments develop and transfer new knowledge between systems and integrate this knowledge in such a way that it becomes workable for creating new products and/or processes. Polis logic is totally dependent on physical proximity in the agora to promote the development of such environments.

Technopoles may exist as separate geographical units within the polis, and have their own agora. Such key technopoles have emerged globally: Singapore, Paris–south, London–M4 corridor, Milan, Moscow–Zelenograd, Boston Route 128, Silicon Valley, Seattle, etc. However, a technopolis is just one type of polis; there are also other types of polises and their agora related to the areas of economics, culture and politics. Polis logic presupposes a concentration of a large number of individuals who have similar mindsets. It is also related to a high degree of risk-taking. However, when risks are taken in the polis, if one is unsuccessful, the polis still provides many new opportunities for finding a new project or job, so risk-taking will not be hampered by the fear of failure. Thus, the polis provides a protective framework around risk-taking, resulting in a willingness to change and a high degree of innovation, which will be the hallmark of the polis. Innovation, spin-offs and creativity will characterize polis areas. In turn, this will reinforce the influx into these areas, because they will have a magnetic effect on young people and knowledge workers.

The simultaneous existence of stability and change will also become a hall-mark of polis areas. In the polis environments that have already been established, as mentioned above, we see a lot of job changing. There will emerge a distinction between jobs that change and work that continues. To be out of a job is not so bad, as long as one has work to do.

The distinction between jobs and work increases the dynamics of the polis areas. Despite changing jobs, people will still be able to work with a project as an entrepreneur, etc. It's only the address of the office that changes, when there is a shift between jobs and work.

Polis logic is not driven separately by local or global dynamics, but is a fusion of global and local thinking, embodied in a modular network logic that enables a global environment to develop in the local polises. The dynamics between the various polises is essential for maintaining a high degree of innovation in the individual polises. The concentration of people in the polis, and the simultaneous multicultural synthesis created in the meeting between polises worldwide, the global part of the polis logic, will maintain innovation opportunities in the local polises. This may be said to be the global variation of the strength of weak ties, and the explanation of the distinction between jobs and work. Jobs change extremely in the Fourth Industrial Revolution, but work is continuous.

Note

1 https://en.wikipedia.org/wiki/Megacity, more than 10 million people.

References

Abd, K.K. (2017). Intelligent sheduling of robotic flexible assembly cells, Springer, London.

Abrahamson, M. (2004). Global cities, Oxford University Press, Oxford.

Ali, T. (2015). The extreme centre, Verso, London.

Applebaum, E. & Batt, R. (1993). The new American workplace, Cornell University Press, Ithaca, NY.

Armano, E. & Murgia, A. (2015). The precariousnesses of young knowledge workers: A subject-oriented aproach, in Johnson, M (Ed.) Precariat: Labour, work and politics, Routledge, London, pp.102–117.

Armstrong, M. (2014a). Armstrong's handbook of strategic human resource management, Kogan Page, New York.

Armstrong, M. (2014b). Armstrong's handbook of human resource management practice, Kogan Page, New York.

Avent, R. (2016). The wealth of humans: Work and its absence in the twenty-first century, Allen Lane, New York.

Barrat, J. (2015). Our final invention, St Martin's Griffin, London.

Bateson, G. (1972). Steps to an ecology of mind, Ballantine Books, New York.

Bauman, Z. (2011). Culture in a liquid modern world, Polity Press, London.

Bauman, Z. (2013). Does the richness of the few benefit us all? Polity, London.

Bennis, W.G., Cloke, K. & Goldsmith, J. (2012). The end of management and the rise of organizational democracy, John Wiley & Sons, New York.

Bleuer, H., Bouri, M. & Mandada, F.C. (2017). New trends in medical and service robots, Springer, London.

Bolanski, L. & Chiapello, E. (2017). The new spirit of capitalism, Verso, London.

Bratianu, C. (2015). Organizational knowledge dynamics, Information Science Reference, New York.

Brynjolfsson, E. & McAfee, A. (2011). Race against the machine, Digital Frontier Press, New York.

Brynjolfsson, E. & McAfee, A. (2014). The second machine age, W.W. Norton & Company, New York.

Brynjolfsson, E. & Saunders, A. (2013). Wired for innovation: How information technology is reshaping the economy, The MIT Press, London.

Budd, L. & Whimster, S. (red.) (1992). Global finance and urban living: A study of metropolitan change, Routledge, London.

Cao, Q., Simsek, Z. & Zhang, H. (2010). Modelling the joint impact of the CEO and the TM Ton organizational ambidexterity, Journal of Management Studies, 47: 1272–1296.

Cappelin, R. (Ed.) (1991). Innovation networks: Spatial perspectives, Behaven Press, London.

Carayannopoulos, S. (2009). How technology-based new firms leverage newness and smallness to commercialize disruptive technologies, Entrepreneurship Theory and Practice, 33, 2: 419–438.

Case, S. (2016). The third wave, Simon & Schuster, New York.

Castelfranchi, C. (2007). Six critical remarks on science and the construction of the knowledge society, Journal of Science Communication, 6, 4: 1–3.

Castells, M. (1989). The informational city: Information technology, economic restructuring and the urban-regional process, Blackwell, Oxford.

Castells, M. (2009a). The power of identity, Wiley-Blackwell, Oxford.

Castells, M. (2009b). The rise of the network society, Wiley-Blackwell, Oxford.

Castells, M. (2016). Network of outrage and hope: Social movements in the internet age, Polity Press, New York.

Catmull, E. (2014). Creativity inc, Bantam Books, New York.

Certomá, C., Dyer, M. & Pocatilu, L. (2017). Citizen empowerment and innovation in the data-rich city, Springer, London.

Champy, J. (1995). Reengineering management, Harper Business, New York.

Chandraekaren, A., Linderman, K. & Schraeder, R. (2012). Antecedents to ambidexterity competency in high technology organizations, Journal of Operations Management, 30: 134–151.

Chang, S.-J. (2008). Sony vs. Samsung: The inside story of the electronic giants battle for global supremacy, John Wiley & Sons, Singapore.

Charnock, G. & Starosta, G. (2016). The new international division of labour: Global transformation and uneven development, Palgrave, London.

Chomsky, N. (2012). How the world works, Hamish Hamilton, London.

Chomsky, N. (2016a). Who rules the world?, Hamish Hamilton, London.

Chomsky, N. (2016b). Profit over people: War against people, Piper, Berlin.

Coates, K.S. & Morrison, B. (2016). Dream factories, Dundum, London.

Denis, E. & Zérah, M.-H. (2017). Subaltern urbanisation in India: An introduction to the dynamics of ordinary towns, Springer, London.

Dickinson, E. (2016). Globalization and migration, Rowman & Littlefield, London.

Doeringer, P.B. (1991). Turbulence in the American workplace, Oxford University Press, New York.

Dorling, D. (2015). Inequality and the 1%, Verso, London.

Evans, D.S. & Schmalensee, R. (2016). Matchmakers, Harvard Business Review Press, Boston, MA.

Frey, C.B. & Osborne, M.A. (2013). The future of employment: How susceptible are jobs to computerization? Oxford Martin School Press, Oxford.

Furnham, A. (1997) The psychology of behaviour at work, Psychology Press, Sussex.

Garud, R., Kumaraswamy, A. & Langlois, R (2002). Managing in the modular age: New perspectives on architectures, networks and organizations, Wiley-Blackwell, New York.

Godard, J. (2010). What is best for workers? The implication of workplace and human resource management practices revisited, Industrial Relations, 49, 3: 466–488.

Graham, S. (1994). Networking cities: Telematics in urban policy – A critical review, International Journal of Urban Regional Research, 18, 3: 416–431.

Graham, S. & Marvin, S. (1996). Telecommunications and the city: Electronic spaces, urban places, Routledge, London.

Gupta, S., Habjan, J. & Tutek, H. (2016). Academic labour unemployment and global higher education: Neoliberal politics of funding and management, Palgrave, London.

Hage, J. & Powers, C.H. (1992). Post-industrial lives. Roles and relations in the 21st century, Sage, London.

Hamel, G. (2008). Introduction, in Skarzynski, P. & Gibson, R Innovation to the core, Harvard Business Press, Boston, MA, pp.xvii–xix.

Hamel, G. (2012). What matters now: How to win in a world of relentless change ferocious competition, and unstoppable innovation, John Wiley & Sons, New York.

Harrison, B. (1994). Lean and mean, Basic Books, New York.

Harvey, T.R. (2010). Resistance to change, R & L Education, London.

Henderson, J. (1989). The globalization of high technology production: Society, space and semiconductors in the restructuring of the modern world, Routledge, London.

Henderson, J. (1990). The American semiconductor industry and the new international division of labour, Routledge, London.

Hlupic, V. (2014). The management shift, Palgrave Macmillan, New York.

Innerarity, D. (2012). Power and knowledge: The politics of the knowledge society, European Journal of Social Theory, 16, 1: 3–16.

Jemielniak, D. (2012). The new knowledge workers, Edward Elgar, Cheltenham.

Jemielniak, D. (2014). The laws of the knowledge workplace, Gower, London.

Jiang, K., Lepak, D.P., Hu, J. & Baer, J.C. (2012). How does human resource management influence organizational outcomes? A meta-analytic investigation of mediating mechanisms, Academy of Management Journal, 55, 6: 1264–1294.

Johannessen, J.-A. (2016). Innovations leads to economic crises: Explaining the bubble economy, Palgrave, London.

Malkin, C. (2016). Rethinking narcissism: The secret to recognising and coping with narcissists, Harper, New York.

Mason, P. (2015). Postcapitalism: A guide to our future, Allen Lane, London.

McGill, K. (2016). Global inequality, University of Toronto Press, Toronto.

Meister, J.C. & Mulcahy, K.J. (2017). The future workplace experience, McGraw Hill, New York.

Mieg, H.A. & Tøpfer, K. (Eds.) (2013). Institutional and social innovation for sustainable urban development, Routledge, London.

Noonan, N.C. & Nadkarny, V. (2016). Challenge and change, Palgrave, London.

Pelling, M. & Blackburn, S. (Eds.) (2013). Megacities and the coast, Routledge, London.

Piketty, T. (2014). Capital in the twenty-first century, The Belknap Press of Harvard University Press, Boston, MA.

Pink, D. (2001). Free agent Nation: The future of working for yourself, Grand Central Publishing, New York.

Roat, H. (2016). Capital and collusion: The political logic of global economic development, Princeton University Press, Princeton, NJ.

Rodrik, D. (2011). The globalization paradox, Oxford University Press, Oxford.

Rosa, H. & Mathys-Treio, J. (2015). Social acceleration, Columbia University Press, New York.

Rothkopf, D. (2009). Superclass: The global power elite and the world they are making, Strauss and Giroux, New York.

Sanseverino, E.R. & Sanseverino, R.R. (2017). Smart cities: Western and eastern intelligent communities, Springer, London.

Sassen, S. (1991). The global city: New York, London, Tokyo, Princeton University Press, Princeton, NJ.

Sassen, S. (2002). Global networks/linked cities, Routledge, New York.

Savage, M. (2015). Social class in the 21st century, Penguin, London.

Schwab, K. (2016). The fourth industrial revolution, World Economic Forum, Geneva.

Sennett, R. (2006). The culture of the new capitalism, Yale University Press, London.

Sennett, R. (2009). The craftsman, Penguin, New York.

Sennett, R. (2013). Together, Penguin, New York.

Srinivasa, R. (2017). Whose global village?: Rethinking how technology shapes the world, New York University Press, London.

Standing, G. (2014a). The precariat: The new dangerous class, Bloomsburry Academic, New York.

Standing, G. (2014b). A precariat charter, Bloomsbury, London.

Weick, K.E. (1979). The social psychology of organizing, Longman, New York.

Wilkinson, R. & Pickett, K. (2009). The spirit level: Why greater equality makes societies stronger, Bloomsbury Press, London.

Wilson, M. (2017). Implementation of robot systems, Butterworth-Heineman, New York.

Zhao, J., Feng, Z., Chu, F. & Ma, N. (2017). Advanced theory of constraint and motion analysis for robot mechanisms, Academic Press, London.

5 Concepts

Ambidextrous organizations

Ambidextrous organizations are organizations that have the ability to adapt to changes in external conditions while at the same time generating their own future by means of, among other things, performance improvement, growth and innovation (Duncan, 1976; O'Reilly & Tushman, 2004, 2006, 2011; Thota & Munir, 2011).

In 2004, O'Reilly and Tushman expressed that ambidextrous organizations would constitute one of the major challenges for management in the global knowledge economy.

The findings of O'Reilly and Tushman (2004) were overwhelming. With regard to the launching of radical innovations, they found that none of the cross-functional or unsupported teams, and only a quarter of the teams with functional designs, could produce radical innovations, whereas, among the ambidextrous organizations, 90 per cent were successful in producing radical innovations. Empirical research has shown that this type of organizational design is best for producing both incremental and radical innovations (Thota & Munir, 2011).

Asplund's motivation theory[1]

In brief, this theory can be described in the following way: 'People are motivated by social responses' (Asplund, 2010: 221–229). The following statement may be said to be a central point made by Asplund's theory: 'When people receive social responses, their level of activity increases.'

Asplund's motivation theory is consistent with North's action theory (see North's action theory). Understood in this way, it seems reasonable to connect the two theories in the statement: 'People are motivated by the social responses rewarded by the institutional framework.'

Availability cascades

This refers to the idea that we are all controlled by the image of reality created by the media, because this image is easy to retrieve from memory.

Availability proposition

This may be expressed as follow: the more easily information enters our consciousness, the greater the likelihood that we will have confidence in that information. In other words, we believe more in the type of information that is available in memory than information that is not so readily available.

Behavioural perspective

This perspective focuses on the behaviour of employees as an explanation for the relationship between business strategy and the results obtained.

Boudon–Coleman diagram

This research methodology was developed by Mario Bunge (1979: 76–79) based on insights made by the sociologists Boudon and Coleman. The purpose of the diagram is to show the relationship between the various levels, such as the macro- and micro-levels. For instance, it is shown how changes at the macro-level, such as technological innovations in feudal society, can lead to increased income at the micro-level. However, it was shown that technological innovations could lead to weakening of the semi-feudal structures because dependency on landowners was reduced. Consequently, the landowners opposed such changes, especially in the case of technological innovations, which Boudon has shown in his research (Boudon, 1981: 100). Coleman (Coleman, 1990: 7–12) started at the macro-level, went to the individual level to find explanations and finally ended up at the macro-level again.

An important purpose of Bunge's Boudon–Coleman diagram is to identify social mechanisms that maintain or change the phenomenon or problem under investigation (as mentioned above, in Boudon's analysis of semi-feudal society). Bunge's Boudon–Coleman diagram may be said to represent a 'mixed strategy'; Bunge says the following:

> When studying systems of any kind a) reduce them to their components (at some level) and the interaction among these, as well as among them and environmental items, but acknowledge and explain emergence (see the chapter on concepts) whenever it occurs, and b) approach systems from all pertinent sides and on all relevant levels, integrating theories or even research fields whenever unidisciplinarity proves to be insufficient.
>
> (Bunge, 1998: 78).

The purpose of this research strategy is to arrive at a deeper and more complete explanation of a system's behaviour.

Capabilities

Capabilities for an organization are what abilities are for an individual. An organizational capability may thus be defined as an organization's ability to perform a task, activity or process. Operational capabilities enable an organization to make money in the here and now (Winter, 2003: 991–995). Dynamic capabilities, as opposed to operational capabilities, are linked to processes of change. Change and innovation are at the centre of dynamic capabilities.

Simplified, one may say that organizational capabilities are something an organization does well compared with its competitors (Ulrich & Brockbank, 2005). These capabilities are intangible and therefore difficult for competitors to imitate (Wernerfelt, 1984).

Cohesive energy

In a social system cohesive energy is 'the glue' that binds the system together. Cohesive energy is the social mechanisms that make the system durable. According to systemic thinking it is the relationships and actions that bind social systems together. The rationale is that relationships and systems of relationships may be said to control human behaviour. Social systems are held together (in systemic thinking) by dynamic social relationships (e.g. feelings, perceptions, norms) and social action (e.g. cooperation, solidarity, conflict and communication).

Co-creation

Co-creation involves working together to promote knowledge processes and innovation. If knowledge processes and innovation are essential for value creation in the knowledge society, co-creation is an important social mechanism for initiating, maintaining and strengthening these processes. The balance between competition and cooperation, embodied in the concept of co-creation, leads to constructive criticism and the necessary scope of knowledge that exists in the network so as to promote creativity and innovation. Instead of a zero-sum situation, a positive-sum situation will be developed in which everyone wins.

Collective blindness

Collective blindness may be said to be a form of collective arrogance, which results in irrational actions. Minor events slip under the radar, causing the system not to be fully aware of what is happening. Politicians' explanations of why voters in a referendum vote contrary to what most of the power élite and the media advocated is an example of collective blindness.

Competence

Competence refers to knowledge, skills and attitudes.

Core competence

The concept was popular in the strategy literature of the 1990s. Core competence may be defined as: 'a bundle of skills and technologies that enable a company to provide a particular benefit to customers' (Hamel & Prahalad, 1996: 219). More recently, core competence as a concept has been given less attention in the research on dynamic capabilities, and now there is more focus on the concept of *fitness*. The term 'evolutionary fitness' is also used in the research literature in connection with technology, quality, cost development, market development, innovation and competitive positioning (Helfat et al., 2007: 7).

Discontinuous innovations

These are innovations that change the premises of technology, markets, our mindset, and so on. We know that sooner or later discontinuous innovations will emerge (Hewing, 2013).

Dynamic capabilities

Dynamic capabilities stem from the resource-based perspective and evolutionary thinking in strategy literature (Nelson & Winter, 1982; Teece, 2013: 3–65, 82–113). The dynamic perspective attempts to explain what promotes an organization's competitive position over time through innovation and growth (Teece, 2013: x).

The original thinking concerning dynamic capabilities may be related to Teece et al. (1997), who defined dynamic capabilities as 'an organization's ability to create, develop and modify its internal and external expertise in order to address changes in the external world'.

Dynamic capabilities are now seen as all the organizational processes, not just internal and external expertise, that contribute to an organization's capacity to adapt to change while creating the organization's future.

Emergent

An emergent occurs if something new turns up on one level that has not previously existed on the level below. With emergent we mean:

> Let S be a system with composition A, i.e. the various components in addition to the way they are composed. If P is a property of S, P is emergent with regard to A, if and only if no components in A possess P; otherwise P is to be regarded as a resulting property with regards to A.
>
> (Bunge, 1977: 97)

Entrepreneurial spirit

The entrepreneurial spirit may be described as follows (Roddick, 2003: 106–107):

- The vision of something new and a belief in this that is so strong that belief becomes reality;
- A touch of positive madness;
- The ability to stand out from the crowd;
- Creative tension bubbling over;
- Pathological optimism;
- To act before you know!
- Basic desire for change;
- Creative energy focused on ideas, not on explicit factual knowledge;
- Being able to tell the story you want to sell.

Evidence

This may be results, such as research results, that can be relied on. However, it is also important to be aware of the fact that other evidence may be available without having to refer to figures and quantities, such as evidence that emerges from observations and good judgement without the assessment being quantified. Evidence-based research is research results that are based on approved and accepted scientific research methods.

Explicit knowledge

This is knowledge that can be digitized and communicated to others as information.

Feedback

Giving the other person feedback, e.g. with regard to their behaviour, attitudes, and the like, is the most important element in the area of interactive skills and emotional intelligence (Goleman, 1996, 2007). Analysis of feedback is a sure way to identify our strengths and then reinforce them (Wang et al., 2003). Failure to give people feedback on their behaviour in some contexts may even be considered immoral.

Feed-forward

Feed-forward is regarded here as an expectation mechanism. It seems reasonable to assume that our expectations influence our behaviour in the present. It is therefore important that we make explicit to ourselves the expectations we have of a situation. By making expectations explicit, we have a greater opportunity to learn from our experiences and thus improve our performance.

Frontline focus

This refers to those in the frontline, i.e. in direct contact with customers, users, patients, students, etc. They have the greatest expertise, necessary information and decision-making authority, and are regarded as the most important resource in the organization because they are at the point where an organization's value creation occurs.

Global competence network

These competence networks may be divided into political, social, economic, technological and cultural patterns. It is when these five patterns interact that one may perceive the overall pattern. In the global knowledge economy it seems reasonable to assume that those who control this pattern set the conditions for economic development. These global competence networks will most likely make an impact on human resource (HR) departments in companies competing for this kind of expertise in national markets.

Global competence networks are also emphasized as crucial for economic growth by the Organisation for Economic Co-operation and Development (OECD, 2001), although they use the term 'innovative clusters'. The purpose of innovative clusters and global competence networks is the development, dissemination and use of new ideas that promote wealth creation.

There is much to suggest that a greater degree of integration and cooperation between private and public sectors, at national and regional levels, is an important prerequisite for initiating the innovative locomotive effect. The global competence networks are metaphorically the energy source that sustains the motion of this locomotive. It would be counterproductive to replace the locomotive once in motion. Conversely, the individual carriages of the locomotive (read: organizational level) can be changed depending on their competitive position. The individual passengers on the train create ideas and knowledge through the processes that may be called *creative chaos*. In this way we will arrive at the three prerequisites for global competence networks: at the individual level, creative chaos occurs; at the organizational level, there will be creative destruction; and at the social and global levels, creative collaboration takes place. These three processes create innovation and economic growth as an emergent, not a *future perfectum*, i.e. a planned process with given results.

A prerequisite for the reasoning above is that tension and competition at one level require collaboration at another level. Competition and cooperation are both necessary if one is to develop innovation and economic growth, in the same manner that stability and change are necessary for flexibility. Too much of the one (stability) leads to rigidity, and too much of the other (change) leads to chaos. Understood in this way, emergents cannot be planned.

Hamel's law of innovation

The 'law' states that only between one and two of a thousand ideas become innovations in a market (Hamel, 2002, 2012). Therefore, an infostructure must be created to ensure that ideas are continuously produced in a business.

Hidden knowledge

Hidden knowledge is what we do not know we do not know. Kirzner (1982) says that hidden knowledge is possibly the most important knowledge domain of creativity, innovation and entrepreneurship.

History's 'slow fields'

This refers to the fact that norms, values and actions tend to be in operation long after the functions, activities and processes that initially created them disappear, thus generating so-called *slow fields of history*. These norms, values and actions exist although they have no apparent function, contributing to maintaining a type of behaviour long after the type of behaviour is functional or meaningful.[2] For sociologists and historians it is important to determine whether norms and values have any function, or whether they are part of history's slow fields. By examining history's slow fields, it may be possible to provide better explanations for phenomena.

HR management

HR management is defined as HR practices at various levels (micro, meso, macro) for managing people in organizations.

HR management has been defined in many different ways, e.g. Boxall & Purcell (2003: 1) define HR management as all those activities oriented towards managing relationships between employees in an organization. This definition emphasizes the relational perspective. Later, they expanded their definition to include all the activities and processes that underpin an organization's value creation (Boxall & Purcell, 2010: 29). On this basis, Armstrong defines the activities and processes that HR management should engage in:

> HRM covers activities such as human capital management, knowledge management, organizational design and development, resource planning (recruitment, talent development), performance management, organizational learning, reward systems, relationships between employees, and employees' wellness.
>
> (Armstrong, 2014: 6).

However, we believe Armstrong underestimates two essential areas of knowledge in his definition: the management of innovation processes, and change processes in organizations. Innovation and change are strongly emphasized in the global HR management survey (White & Younger, 2013: 35–39). Armstrong has included the ethical perspective in his *Handbook for Human Resources Management* (Armstrong, 2014a: 95–105). Management of innovation processes and change processes in organizations is also highlighted and underlined by Wright et al. (2011: 5) in their description of HR management. However, it must also be said that Armstrong discusses innovation (Armstrong, 2014: 145–155), but not in his process definition of HR management. Innovation and change processes are also emphasized by Ulrich et al. (2013). Brockbank (2013: 24) in particular mentions these two processes as being important in the research model that Ulrich et al. (2013) have developed through 25 years of their empirical research.

Implicit knowledge

This is knowledge that is spread throughout an organization but not integrated.

Informats

By informats, we mean robots with artificial intelligence (AI) that are interconnected in a global technological network. Figuratively, informats may be imagined as clusters of neurons in the human brain, which are connected to other neuron clusters to create the various functions of human intelligence (Winfield, 2012; Wilson, 2017; Vadakkepat & Goswami, 2018). In the financial world, the use of robots by financial analysts provides an example of the use of so-called informats. Informats for use in medical surgery are already on the drawing board and will be a reality in the near future (Bleuer et al., 2017); the same applies to the use of informats in the service and education sectors (Bleuer & Bouri, 2017). Informats are understood here in the context of the above description as being emergents[3] in relation to robots; informats can sense, analyse and reach decisions in the space of a micro-second.

Information input overload

This occurs when an individual, a team, an organization or a community receives more information than they can manage to process.

In a situation characterized by information input overload, the following may occur (Miller, 1978: 123):

1. Designated tasks and responsibilities are left undone;
2. Errors are made;
3. Queues of information occur;
4. Information is filtered out that should have been included;
5. Abstract formulations are made when they should have been specific;
6. Communication channels are overloaded, creating stress and tension in the system;

7. Complex situations are shunned;
8. Information is lumped together for processing.

   Each of the above eight points may result in a decrease in efficiency when the system is exposed to information input overload.

Infostructure

The infostructure concerns the processes that enable the development, transfer, analysis, storage, coordination and management of data, information and knowledge. The infostructure consists of eleven generic processes, which may be considered as nodes in a social network at different levels, e.g. team, organization, society and region, all in the global space. Together, the eleven processes comprise the totality of the infostructure.

   It may be said that the *info*structure has the same importance in the knowledge society as the *infra*structure had in the industrial society.

Innovation

Innovation is here understood as any idea, practice or material element that is perceived as new to the person using it (Zaltman et al., 1973).

   Ideas are seen as the smallest unit in the innovation process (Hamel, 2002, 2012). However, this refers to the ideas that are in the development process rather than fully developed ideas. Before an idea can be characterized as innovative, it must prove beneficial to somebody, i.e. the market must accept the idea and apply it. Consequently, the creative process of innovation is here understood as the benefit it has for a market (Amabile, 1990; Johannessen et al., 2001: 25). Thus, it is not sufficient for an idea to be new for it to be considered an innovation. An idea may have a great degree of novelty, but, if it is of no benefit to anybody in the market, then it has no innovative value.

Kaizen

This is a Japanese method, which means that an organization develops systems for organized improvement (Maurer, 2012).

Knowledge

The definition of knowledge used here is *the systematization and structuring of information for one or more goals or purposes.*

Knowledge worker

A knowledge worker has been described by the OECD as *a person whose primary task is to generate and apply knowledge*, rather than to provide services or produce physical products (OECD, 2000a, 2000b, 2000c, 2000d, 2000e, 2001). This may be understood as a *formal definition* of a knowledge worker.

This definition does not restrict knowledge workers to creative fields, as is the case with, for example, the work of Mosco and McKercher (2007: vii–xxiv). The OECD definition also allows for the fact that a knowledge worker may perform routine tasks, but does not limit the type of work performed by knowledge workers to tasks relating to creative problem-solving strategies, unlike the definition provided by Reinhardt et al. (2011).

Knowledge enterprise

This is an enterprise that has knowledge as its most significant output. It is perhaps helpful to think of the process *input–process–output* to separate industrial enterprises from knowledge enterprises. A great deal of knowledge and skills are needed to produce high-tech products such as computers, and there are also many knowledge workers involved in this process. However, most of the products produced today are high-tech industrial products and, although such products require very skilled knowledge in the production process, they are nevertheless output–industrial products.

On the other hand, law firms, consulting firms and universities are examples of knowledge enterprises.

Knowledge management

This is management of knowledge resources in an organization. These resources may be explicit knowledge, implicit knowledge, tacit knowledge or hidden knowledge.

Locomotive effect

This refers to something that generates and then reinforces an activity or development.

Modularization

An extreme fragmentation of the production process in the global knowledge economy. Production is fragmented and distributed according to the following logic: costs–quality–competence–design–innovation.

Modular flexibility

This is the modulization of value creation. Modular flexibility may best be understood as the globalization of production processes, and extreme specialization of work processes with a focus on core processes.

Necessary and sufficient conditions

It may often be appropriate to divide conditions or premises into *necessary conditions* and *sufficient conditions*. Necessary conditions must be present to trigger an action, but these may not be sufficient. The sufficient conditions must also be present to trigger the action.

North's action theory[4]

This action theory may be expressed in the following statement: 'People act on the basis of a system of rewards as expressed in the norms, values, rules and attitudes in the culture (the institutional framework)' (North, 1990, 1993). North's action theory is also consistent with Asplund's motivation theory (see Asplund's motivation theory).

Primary task

An organization's primary task is what the system is designed to do.

Proposition

This is an overarching hypothesis. It says something about the interrelationship of several variables. A proposition relates to a hypothesis in the same way the main research problem relates to research questions.

Punctuation

By punctuation (Bateson, 1972: 292–293) a distinction is drawn between cause and effect; this is done with a clear motive in mind. A causality is thus created, which does not actually exist in the real world, and one is then free to discuss the effects of this cause which has been created through a process of punctuation.

A sequence of a process is selected, and then bracketed. In this way, we delimit what is punctuated from the rest of the process. Figuratively, we may imagine this as a circle that is divided into small pieces; one piece of the circle is then selected and unfolded into a straight line. This results in the creation of an artificial beginning and end. This beginning and end of course cannot exist in a circle, but only through the process of punctuation.

Social laws

Social laws constitute a pattern of a unique type. They are systemic and connected to a system of knowledge, and cannot change without the facts they represent also being changed (Bunge, 1983a, 1983b). The main differences between a statement of a law and other statements are:

1. Law statements are general;
2. Law statements are systemic, i.e. they are related to the established system of knowledge;
3. Law statements have been verified through many studies.

A pattern may be understood as variables that are stable over a specific period of time. A social law is created when an observer gains insight into the pattern. By gaining such insight, we can also predict parts of behaviour or at least develop a rough estimate within a short period of time.

Social laws are further related to specific social systems, in both time and space. However, this does not represent any objection to social laws, because this is also true of natural laws (although these have a longer timespan and are of a more general nature).

Social mechanism

Robert Merton (1967) brought the notion of social mechanisms into sociology, although we can find rudiments of this in both Weber – with the Protestant ethic as an explanation for the emergence of capitalism in Europe – and Durkheim, who uses society as an explanation for a rising suicide rate. For Merton, social mechanisms are the building blocks of *middle range theories*. He defines social mechanisms as 'social processes having designated consequences for designated parts of the social structure' (Merton, 1967: 43). In the 1980s and 1990s, Jon Elster developed a new notion of the role of social mechanisms in sociology (Elster, 1986, 1989). Hedstrom and Swedberg write that: 'the advancement of social theory calls for an analytical approach that systematically seeks to explicate the social mechanisms that generate and explain observed associations between events' (Hedstrøm & Swedberg, 1998: 1).

It is one thing to point out connections between phenomena, and something quite different to point out satisfactory explanations for these relationships, which is what social mechanisms accomplish. A social mechanism tells us what will happen, how it will happen and why it will happen (Bunge, 1967). Social mechanisms are primarily analytical constructs that cannot necessarily be observed; in other words, they are epistemological, not ontological. However, social mechanisms are observable in their consequences. An intention can be a social mechanism of action. We cannot observe an intention, but we can interpret it in the light of the consequences manifested through an action. Preferences can also function as a social mechanism for economic behaviour. We cannot observe a person's preferences, but we can interpret them in the light of the behavioural consequences that manifest themselves. Understood in this way, social mechanisms are analytical constructs, indicating connections between events (Hernes, 1998).

Bunge says: 'a social mechanism is a process in a concrete system, such that it is capable of being about or preventing some change in the system as a whole or in some of its subsystems' (Bunge, 1997a: 414). By 'social mechanism' here we mean those activities that promote/inhibit social processes in relation to a specific problem/phenomenon.

Material resources and technology are social mechanisms of the economic subsystem; power is a social mechanism of the political subsystem; fundamental norms and values are a social mechanism of the cultural subsystem; and human relationships are a social mechanism of the social subsystem. These system-specific social mechanisms interact with each other to achieve certain goals, maintain these systems or avoid certain undesirable conditions in the system or the outside world.

The difficulty of discovering social mechanisms and distinguishing them from processes may be partly explained by the fact that social mechanisms are also processes (Bunge, 1997a: 414). For the application of social mechanisms, see the Boudon–Coleman diagram.

Social system

From a systemic perspective, social systems can be conceptual or concrete. Theories and analytical models are examples of conceptual systems. Further-more, social systems are *composed of people and their artefacts* (Bunge, 1996: 21). Social systems are held together (in systemic reasoning) by **dynamic social relations** (such as emotions, interpretations, norms, etc.) and **social actions** (such as cooperation, solidarity, conflict and communication). None of the social actions has precedence in the systemic interpretation of social systems, such as conflict in the case of Marx and solidarity in the case of Durkheim.

Staccato behaviour (erratic behaviour)

If organizations introduce too many change processes in succession too quickly, a phenomenon may occur called 'staccato behaviour'.

If an organization does not deal with this appropriately, it seems reasonable to assume that workers will become tired, burnt-out and de-motivated. Perhaps most damaging to business, employees will lose focus on their primary task – what the business is designed to do. In addition, businesses will often experience this leading to an increasing degree of opportunistic behaviour (Ulrich, 2013: 260).

Strategic HR management

Strategic HR management is defined in this book as: 'The choices an HR department makes with regard to human resources for the purposes of achiev-ing the organization's goals.' This is analogous to the view of Storey et al. (2009: 3) and consistent with the definition we employ for HR management. This means that strategic HR management must be focused on the *micro-, meso-* and *macro-levels*.

There are many definitions of strategic HR management, e.g. 'use of human resources in order to achieve lasting competitive advantages for the business' (Mathis & Jackson, 2008: 36); 'development of a consistent practices in order to support the strategic goals of the business' (Mello, 2006: 152); and 'a complex system with the following characteristics: vertical integration, horizontal integration, efficiency, partnership' (Schuler & Jackson, 2005).

Systemic thinking

Systemic thinking distinguishes the epistemological sphere (Bunge, 1985), the ontological sphere (Bunge, 1983a), the axiological sphere (Bunge, 1989, 1996) and the ethical sphere (Bunge, 1989). Systemic thinking makes a clear distinction between intention and behaviour. Intention is something that should be *understood*, whereas behaviour is something that should be *explained*. To understand an intention we must study the historical factors, situations and contexts, as well as the expectation mechanisms. Behaviour must be explained with respect to the context, relationships and situation in which it unfolds. What implication does the distinction between intention and behaviour have for the study of social systems?

Interpretation of meaning is an important part of the *intention aspect* in the distinction. Explanation and prediction become an essential part of the *behavioural aspect* of the distinction.

In systemic thinking it is the link between the interpretation of meaning and explanation, and prediction, that provides historical and social sciences with practical strength. By making a distinction between intention and behaviour, the historical and the social sciences are interpretive, explanatory and predictive projects. According to systemic thinking, many of the contradictions in the historical and social sciences spring from the fact that a distinction is not made between intention and behaviour. The problem of the historical and social sciences is that the actors who are studied both have intentions and exercise types of behaviour; however, this isn't problematic as long as we make a distinction between intention and behaviour. By simultaneously introducing the distinction between intention and behaviour, systemic thinking has made it possible to identify, for instance, partial explanations for each of two main epistemological positions, namely the naturalists and the anti-naturalists (Johannessen & Olaisen, 2005, 2006), and synthesize these explanations into new knowledge.

Systemic thinking emphasizes circular causal processes, also called *interactive causal processes*, in addition to linear causal processes (Johannessen, 1996, 1997). Systemic thinking argues that, to understand objective social facts, one must examine their subjective aspects. In systemic thinking, objective social facts exist, but they are often more difficult to grasp than facts in the natural world, because social facts are often influenced by expectations, emotions, prejudices, ideology, and economic and social interests. '*Aspect-seeing*' is thus a way of approaching these social facts.

Emergents are central to systemic thinking. A pattern behind the problem or phenomenon is always sought in systemic investigations. Patterns may be revealed by studying the underlying processes that constitute a phenomenon or problem, *and the search for pattern is what scientific research is all about* (Bunge, 1996: 42).

According to systemic thinking it is a misconception to say that the facts are social constructions. The misunderstanding involves confusing our *concepts* about facts and our *hypotheses* about the facts together with the facts. Our concepts and hypotheses are mental constructs, but the facts are not mental constructs. Social need, for instance, is not a social fact; it is a mental construct of, for instance, starvation. Starvation is a social fact. Social need is a mental or social construction. Not being able to read is a social fact. Illiteracy is, however, a social construction.

A *symbol* should symbolize something, just as a *concept* should delineate something. A *hypothesis* should explain something or express something about relationships. A conceptual *model* should say something about the relationships between concepts. A *theory* should say something about relationships between propositions. Physical or social facts are untouched by all these mental constructions. That one can change social facts through constructs, or that social facts are changed as a social consequence of using constructs, is neither original nor new.

The aim of theoretical research, according to the systemic position, is the construction of systems, i.e. theories (Bunge, 1974: v). The order in systemic research is thus: theory–analysis–synthesis.

In the methodological sphere, the systemic position has its main focus on relationships, in terms of concrete things, ideas and knowledge. Consequently, systemic thinking encourages interdisciplinary and multidisciplinary approaches to problems or phenomena.

The systemic position thus attempts to bridge the gap between methodological individualism and methodological collectivism, which is considered the classic controversy in historical and social sciences.

The perceptions that an observer has about social systems will influence his or her actions, regardless of whether the perceptions are true or fallacious. Systemic investigations, writes Bunge, therefore start 'from individuals embedded in a society that preexists them and watch how their actions affect society and alter it' (Bunge, 1996: 241). For these reasons the study of social systems from a systemic perspective always includes the triad: actors–observers–social systems.

An observer tries to uncover a system's composition, environment and structure. Then the actors' subjective perception of composition, environment and structure is examined. In other words, both the subjective and the objective aspects are studied. When we wish to study changes in social systems, from a systemic point of view, we have to examine the social mechanisms (drivers) that influence changes; both internal and external social mechanisms must be identified. This study takes place within the four subsystems: economic, political, cultural and relational. According to systemic thinking, social changes occur along seven axes:

1. As an *expectation* of new relationships, values, power constellations, technologies and distribution of material resources;
2. As a result of our *beliefs* (mental models) about relationships, values, power constellations, technical and material resources;
3. As a result of *psychological elements*, such as: irritation, crisis, discomfort, unsatisfactory life, unworthy life, loss of well-being, etc.;
4. As a result of *communication* in and between systems;
5. As a result of an *understanding of connections* (contextual understanding);
6. As a result of learning and new *self-knowledge*;
7. As a result of *new ideas* and ways of thinking.

Historiography, from a systemic perspective, has one clear goal: to investigate what happened, where it happened, when it happened, how it happened, why it happened and with what results.

Systemic assumptions related to historiography and social sciences may be expressed in the following (Bunge, 1998: 263):

a. The past has existed;
b. Parts of the past can be known;
c. Every uncovering of the past will be incomplete;
d. New data, techniques, and systemizations and structuring will reveal new aspects of the past;
e. Historical knowledge is developed through new data, discoveries, hypotheses and approaches.

In systemic thinking, if changes are to take place, then the material will sometimes be given precedence; at other times, ideology, ideas and thinking are given precedence. In other contexts, there is a systemic link between the material and ideas that are needed to bring about changes. In such contexts, it is difficult and irrelevant to say what the primary driver is, i.e. the material or ideas; this would be on a par with discussing what came first, the chicken or the egg.

The processes that drive social change, according to a systemic perspective, are the interaction of the economic, political, relational and cultural subsystems. In some situations, one of these four perspectives will prevail, whereas in others it will be one or more of the four subsystems that are the drivers of social change. In many cases, it is precisely the interaction between the four subsystems that leads to social changes.

In this context the systemic perspective may be described by saying that material conditions/energy, such as economic relationships, may provide the ground from which ideologies develop, but that these ideologies in return influence the development of the material. Whether material conditions/energy or ideology comes first is often determined by a historiographical punctuation process (Bateson, 1972: 163).

The systemic perspective balances historical materialism and historical idealism. It assumes that overall social changes are the result of economic, political, social and cultural factors, in addition to the interaction between material conditions/energy and ideas. Furthermore, a systemic perspective views any society as being interwoven into its surroundings (Bunge, 1998: 275). When a historian considers a historical situation – such as the massacre in Van in April 1915 – from this perspective he is trying 'to throw light upon the internal working of a past culture and society' (Stone, 1979: 19).

The systemic position attempts to view the relevant event in a larger context, in order to find 'the patterns which combine' (Bateson, 1972: 273–274), because 'change depends upon feedback loop' (Bateson, 1972: 274). Bunge says about this position: 'By placing the particular in a sequence, adopting a broad perspective the systemist overcomes the idiographic/nomothetic duality, ..., as well as the concomitant narrative/structural opposition' (Bunge, 1998: 275). This means, metaphorically, that the systemic researcher uses a microscope, telescope and a helicopter to investigate patterns over time.

Systemic research strategy is a 'zig-zagging between the micro-meso and macro-levels' (Bunge, 1998: 277). Through a systemic research strategy the researcher has ample opportunities to use a Boudon–Coleman diagram.

Systemic thinking examines four types of changes.[5]

The systemic researcher attempts to explore the interrelationship of the four types of changes. A single event is not in itself necessarily of special interest to the systemic researcher; rather, the focus is on the *system of events* of which the single event is a part.

Type I change

This concerns individuals who change history, such as Genghis Khan, Hitler, Stalin, Mao Zedong, etc.

Type II change

This concerns groups of people acting together who change history. Examples of type II change include the invasion of the Roman Empire by peoples from the north, and the Ottoman expansion into the Balkans between the late 1400s and when the Ottoman Empire was pushed back, partly due to nationalist liberation movements in the early 1900s.

Type III change

This includes changes in history that are caused by natural disasters, such as the volcanic eruption that destroyed Pompeii. Climate change may also be said to an example of a type III change.

Type IV change

This involves a total change in the way of thinking, such as the emergence of new religions, such as Islam, or a new political ideology, such as Marxism.

All the social sciences are used in the systemic position to seek insight and understanding, and explain a phenomenon or problem.

Tacit knowledge

This is knowledge that is difficult to communicate to others as information. It is also very difficult, if at all possible, to digitize.

The knowledge-based perspective

The knowledge-based perspective is defined here as creating, expanding and modifying internal and external competencies to promote what the organization is designed to do (Grant, 2003: 203).

The resource-based perspective

This perspective can be defined as the structuring and systematization of the organization's internal *resources* so it is difficult for competitors to copy them.

Theory

This is here understood as a system of propositions (Bunge, 1974: v).

Notes

1 Asplund's motivation theory, a term we use here, is based on Asplund's research.
2 Asplund (1970: 55) refers to a similar phenomenon when he discusses Simmel. He points out that the norms that may have had a positive function during a historic phase become, in a later phase, dysfunctional.
3 Emergents appear if something new occurs on a level that did not previously exist on the level below. By emergent we mean: 'Let S be a system with composition A, i.e. the various components in addition to the way they are composed. If P is a property of S, P is emergent with regard to A, if and only if no components in A possess P; otherwise P is to be regarded as a resulting property with regards to A' (Bunge, 1977: 97).
4 North's action theory is a term we use here based on North's research.
5 The four types of changes are related to Bateson's (1972: 279–309) work on different types of learning, especially those discussed in his article 'Logical types of learning and communication'.

References

Amabile, T. (1990). Within you, without you: The social psychology of creativity, and beyond, in Runco, M.A. & Albert, R.S. (eds). Theories of creativity, Sage, London, pp.S61–691.
Armstrong, M. (2014). Armstrong's handbook of strategic human resource management practice, Kogan Page, New York.

Armstrong, M. (2014a). Armstrong's handbook of human resource management practice, Kogan Page, New York.

Asplund, J. (1970). Om undran innfør samhället, Argos, Stockholm.

Asplund, J. (2010). Det sociala livets elementära former, Korpen, Stockholm.

Bateson, G. (1972). Steps to an ecology of mind, Intertext Books, London.

Bleuer, H. & Bouri, M. (2017). New trends in medical and service robots: Assistive, surgical and educational robotics, Springer, London.

Bleuer, H., Bouri, M. & Mandada, F.C. (2017). New trends in medical and service robots, Springer, London.

Boudon, R. (1981). The logic of social action, Routledge, London.

Boxall, P.F. & Purcell, J. (2003). Strategy and human resource management, Palgrave Macmillan, Basingstoke.

Boxall, P.F. & Purcell, J. (2010). An HRM perspective on employee participation, in Wilkinson, A., Golan, P.J., Marchington, M. & Lewins, D. (eds.). The Oxford handbook of participation in organizations, Oxford University Press, Oxford, pp.129–151.

Brockbank, W. (2013). Overview and Logic, in Ulrich, D., Brockbank, W., Younger, J. & Ulrich, M. (eds.). Global HR Competencies: Mastering Competitive Value from the Outside-In, McGraw Hill, New York, 3–27.

Bunge, M. (1967). Scientific Research, Vol. 3, in Studies of the Foundations Methodology and Philosophy of Science, Springer Verlag, Berlin.

Bunge, M. (1974). Sense and Reference, Reidel, Dordrecht.

Bunge, M. (1977). Treatise on Basic Philosophy. Vol. 3. Ontology I: The Furniture of the World, Reidel, Dordrecht.

Bunge, M. (1979). A World of Systems, Reidel, Dordrecht.

Bunge, M. (1983a). Exploring the World: Epistemology & Methodology I, Reidel, Dordrecht.

Bunge, M. (1983b). Understanding the World: Epistemology & Methodology II, Reidel, Dordrecht.

Bunge, M. (1985). Philosophy of Science and Technology. Part I: Epistemology & Methodology III, Reidel, Dordrecht.

Bunge, M. (1989). Ethics: The Good and the Right, Reidel, Dordrecht.

Bunge, M. (1996). Finding Philosophy in Social Science, Yale University Press, New Haven, CT.

Bunge, M. (1997a). Mechanism and explanation, Philosophy of the Social Sciences, 27, 410–465.

Bunge, M. (1998). Philosophy of Science: From Problem to Theory, Vol. 1, Transaction Publishers, New Jersey.

Coleman, J.S. (1990). Foundations of social theory, Harvard University Press, Belknap Press, Cambridge, MA.

Duncan, R. (1976). The Ambidextrual Organization: Designing Dual Structures for Innovation, in Kilman, R.H., Pondy, L.R. & Slevin, D. (eds). The Management of Organization Design, North Holland, New York, pp.167–188.

Elster, J. (1986). Rational choice, New York University Press, New York.

Elster, J. (1989). Nuts and bolts for the social sciences, Cambridge University Press, Cambridge.

Goleman, D. (1996). Emotional intelligence, Bloomsbury Publishing, New York.

Goleman, D. (2007). Social Intelligence, Arrow Books, New York.

Grant, R.M. (2003). The knowledge-based view of the firm, in Faulkner, D. & Campell, A. (eds). The Oxford handbook of strategy, Oxford University Press, Oxford, pp.203–231.

Hamel, G. (2002). Leading the revolution: How to thrive in turbulent times by making innovation a way of life, Harvard Business School Press, Boston, MA.

Hamel, G. (2012). What matters now: How to win in a world of relentless change ferocious competition, and unstoppable innovation, John Wiley & Sons, New York.

Hamel, G. & Prahalad, C.K. (1996). Competing for the future, Harvard Business School Press, Boston, MA.

Hedstrøm, P. & Swedberg, S.R. (1998). Social mechanisms: An introductory essay, in Hedstrøm, P. & R. Swedberg, (eds). Social mechanisms: An analytical approach to social theory, Cambridge University Press, Cambridge.

Helfat, C.E., Finkelstein, S., Mitchell, W., Peteraf, M.A., Singh, H., Teece, D.J. & Winter, S. G. (2007). Dynamic capabilities: Understanding strategic change in organizations, Blackwell, Oxford.

Hernes, G. (1998). Real virtuality, in social mechanisms: An analytical approach to social theory, in Hedstrøm, P. & Swedberg, R. (eds). Social mechanisms: An analytical approach to social theory, Cambridge University Press, Cambridge, pp.74–102.

Hewing, M. (2013). Collaboration with potential users for discontinuous innovation, Springer Gabler, Potsdam.

Johannessen, J.-A. (1996). Systemics applied to the study of organizational fields: Developing systemic research strategy for organizational fields, Kybernetes, 25, 1: 33–51.

Johannessen, J.-A. (1997). Aspects of ethics in systemic thinking, Kybernetes, 26, 9: 983–1001.

Johannessen, J.-A. & Olaisen, J. (2005). Systemic philosophy and the philosophy of social science-Part I: Transcedence of the naturalistic and the anti-naturalistic position in the philosophy of social science, Kybernetes, 34, 7/8: 1261–1277.

Johannessen, J.-A. & Olaisen, J. (2006). Systemic philosophy and the philosophy of social science, Part II: The systemic position, I Kybernetes, 34, 9/10: 1570–1586.

Johannessen, J.-A. Olaisen, J. & Olsen, B. (2001). Mismanagement of tacit knowledge: The importance of tacit knowledge, the danger of information technology, and what to do about it? International Journal of Information Management, 21, 3: 3–20.

Kirzner, S. (1982). The theory of entrepreneurship in economic growth, in Kent, C.A., Sexton, D. L. & Vesper, K.H. (eds). Encyclopedia of entrepreneurship, Prentice Hall, Englewood Cliffs, NJ.

Maurer, K. (2012). The spirit of kaizen, McGraw-Hill, New York.

Mathis, R. & Jackson, J.H. (2008). Human resource management, South Western Cengage Learning, Cincinnati, OH.

Mello, J.A. (2006). Human resource management, South Western Cengage Learning, Cincinnati, OH.

Merton, R.K. (1967). Social theory and social structure, Free Press, London.

Miller, J.G. (1978). Living systems, McGraw-Hill, New York.

Mosco, V. & McKercher, C. (2007). Introduction: Theorizing knowledge labor and the information society, inKnowledge workers in the information society, Lexington Books, Lanham.

Nelson, R.R. & Winter, S.G. (1982). An evolutionary theory of economic change, Harvard University Press, Cambridge, MA.

North, D. (1993). Nobel Lecture: www.nobelprize.org/nobel_prizes/economics/laureates/1993/north-lecture.html#not2, lesedato, 4.5.2012.

North, D.C. (1990). Institutions, institutional change and economic performance, Cambridge University Press, Cambridge.

O'Reilly, C.A. & Tushman, M.L. (2004). The Ambidextrous organization, Harvard Business Review, 82, 4: 74–81.

O'Reilly, C.A. & Tushman, M.L. (2011). Organizational ambidexterity in action: How managers explore and exploit, California Management Review, 53, 4: 5–22.

Organisation for Economic Co-operation and Development (2000a). A new economy? The changing role of innovation and information technology in growth, OECD Paris.

Organisation for Economic Co-operation and Development. (2000b). Economic outlook, OECD Paris.

Organisation for Economic Co-operation and Development. (2000c). Education at a glance: OECD indicators, CERI, Paris.

Organisation for Economic Co-operation and Development. (2000d). ICT skills and employment, working party on the information economy, Paris, 15 November, DSTI/ ICCP/IE (2000)7.

Organisation for Economic Co-operation and Development. (2000e). Knowledge management in the learning society, CERI, Paris.

Organisation for Economic Co-operation and Development. (2001). Innovative clusters: Driving of national innovation-systems, OECD, Paris.

Reinhardt, W., Smith, B., Sloep, P. & Drachler, H. (2011). Knowledge worker roles and actions – results of two empirical studies, Knowledge and Process Management, 18, 3: 150–174.

Roddick, D.A. (2003). The grassroots entrepreneur, Elbæk, U. & Kaospilot, A.Z. (eds). Narayana Press, Gylling.

Schuler, R.S. & Jackson, S.E. (2005). A quarter century review of human resource management in the US: the growth in importance of the international perspective, Management Revue, 16, 1: 11–35.

Stone, J. (1979). The revival of narrative, Reflections on a new old history, past and present, 85, 3–24.

Storey, J., Ulrich, D. & Wright, P.M. (2009). Introduction, in Storey, J., Wright, P.M. & Ulrich, D. (eds). The Routledge companion to strategic human resource management, Routledge, London, pp.3–15.

Teece, D., Pisano, G. & Shuen, A. (1997). Dynamic capabilities and strategic management, Strategic Management Journal, 18, 7: 509–533.

Teece, D.J. (2013). Dynamic capabilities and strategic management: Organizing for innovation, Oxford University Press, Oxford.

Thota, H. & Munir, Z. (2011). Key concepts in innovation, Palgrave Macmillan, London.

Ulrich, D. (2013). Future of global HR: What's next? in Ulrich, D., Brockbank, W., Younger, J. & Ulrich, M. (eds). Global HR competencies: Mastering competitive value from the outside-in, McGraw Hill, New York, 255–268.

Ulrich, D. & Brockbank, W. (2005). The HR value proposition, Harvard Business School Press, Boston, MA.

Ulrich, D., Brockbank, W., Younger, J. & Ulrich, M. (eds). (2013). Global HR competencies: Mastering competitive value from the outside-in, McGraw Hill, New York.

Vadakkepat, P. & Goswami, P. (eds). (2018). Humanoid robotics: A reference, Springer, London.

Wang, Q.-G., Lee, T.H. & Lin, C. (2003). Relay feedback: Analysis, identification and control, Springer, London.

Wernerfelt, B. (1984). A resource-based view of the firm, Strategic Management Journal, 5, 2: 171–180.

White, J. & Younger, J. (2013). The global perspective, in Ulrich, D., Brockbank, W., Younger, J. & Ulrich, M. (eds). Global HR competencies: Mastering competitive value from the outside-in, McGraw Hill, New York, 27–53.

Wilson, M. (2017). Implementation of robot systems, Butterworth-Heinemann, New York.

Winfield, A. (2012). Robotics, Oxford University Press, Oxford.

Winter, S.G. (2003). Understanding dynamic capabilities, Strategic Management Journal, 24, 991–995.

Wright, P.M., Boudreau, J.W., Pace, D.A., Libby Sartain, E., McKinnon, P. & Antoine, R.L. (eds). (2011).The chief HR officer: Defining the new role of human resource leaders, Jossey-Bass, London.

Zaltman, G., Duncan, R. & Holbeck, J. (1973). Innovations and organizations, Wiley, New York.

Index

For Product Safety Concerns and Information please contact our EU representative GPSR@taylorandfrancis.com Taylor & Francis Verlag GmbH, Kaufingerstraße 24, 80331 München, Germany

Printed and bound by CPI Group (UK) Ltd, Croydon, CR0 4YY

01/05/2025

01858414-0009